JOSEPH AND ASENETH
AND THE JEWISH TEMPLE IN HELIOPOLIS

SOCIETY OF BIBLICAL LITERATURE

EARLY JUDAISM AND ITS LITERATURE

Number 10

JOSEPH AND ASENETH
AND THE JEWISH TEMPLE IN HELIOPOLIS

by
Gideon Bohak

JOSEPH AND ASENETH
AND THE JEWISH TEMPLE IN HELIOPOLIS

by
Gideon Bohak

Scholars Press
Atlanta, Georgia

Library of Congress Cataloging-in-Publication Data

Bohak, Gideon, 1961–
    Joseph and Aseneth and the Jewish temple in Heliopolis / by Gideon Bohak.
        p. cm. —(Early Judaism and its literature ; no. 10)
    Includes bibliographical references and index.
    ISBN 0-7885-0179-8 (cloth : alk. paper).
    1. Joseph and Asenath—Criticism, interpretation, etc. 2. Temples—Egypt—Heliopolis (Extinct city) 3. Judaism—Egypt—Heliopolis (Extinct city) I. Title. II. Series.
  BS1830.J62B64   1996
  229'.91—dc20   96-27888
                      CIP

Reprinted in paper 2009, ISBN 978-1-58983-437-8 (paper : alk. paper).

Printed in the United States of America
on acid-free paper

לדבורה

Table of Contents

Acknowledgments

This study is a thoroughly revised edition of the doctoral dissertation I completed at Princeton University in 1994. Having benefited from the constant support and guidance of Martha Himmelfarb and John Gager, I would like to take this opportunity to thank them once again for all that they have done to make this study possible. I am also deeply indebted to Peter Brown, for his inspiration and criticism, and to Erich Gruen, for his detailed and penetrating comments on earlier drafts of my dissertation.

During my work on *Joseph and Aseneth* and on Onias' temple I sought much advice and incurred many debts. I am especially grateful to Ernst Bammel, Gabriele Boccaccini, Christoph Burchard, John Collins, Traianos Gagos, Martin Goodman, Jan Willem van Henten, Edith Humphrey, Janet Johnson, Ludwig Koenen, Bob Kraft, Bob Lamberton, Joe Manning, John Ray, Dorothy Thompson, Stephanie West, and the two anonymous readers of the original manuscript. If my debts to all these scholars and friends become apparent in what follows, my own errors are bound to stand out even more.

In preparing the final manuscript, I was greatly aided by the sharp eyes and disciplined minds of Barbara Ryan and Kathryn Beam. The map was drawn by Karl Longstreth, using ArcView software.

By dedicating this study to Dvorah Janssens, a collaborator and a critic, I wish to thank her for the constant support, patience, and humor, without which all this would never have been possible.

Introduction

Some time in the late sixth century CE, an old book was found in the library of a Syrian episcopal family. The puzzled finder, whose identity remains unknown to us, sent the book to Moses, the Bishop of Aggel, asking him to translate it into Syriac and to interpret its meaning.

Moses was very obliging. He translated the entire book, and offered his Christological, allegorical interpretation of the narrative. Unfortunately, while the two letters and Moses' translation are extant—embedded in Ps.-Zacharias Rhetor's *Historia Ecclesiastica*— the exact details of Moses' allegorical interpretation are irretrievably lost.[1] The book in question, however—commonly known today as *Joseph and Aseneth*—has come down to us not only in its Syriac translation, but also in Greek, Latin, Church Slavonic, and Armenian.[2] It tells the story of Aseneth, the daughter of the high priest of Heliopolis, who is mentioned in the Hebrew Bible only in passing (Gen 41:45, 50; 46:20). Aseneth, the story goes, is a beautiful and arrogant virgin who refuses to marry any man and lives in her own separate tower, adjacent to her parents' house, accompanied by her seven maidservants. When Joseph, Pharaoh's deputy (cf. Gen 41:40-4), comes to Heliopolis, Aseneth is stunned by his beauty and falls madly in love with him, but he pushes her away, refusing even to kiss an idolatrous woman. Shocked and dismayed, she locks herself up in her tower and spends a whole week fasting and crying, repenting of her arrogance and her idolatry, and begging the Most High God to forgive her. Next, an angel appears in her room, and tells her that her repentance has been accepted and that

---

[1] For the Syriac text, and a Latin translation, see E.W. Brooks, *Historia... Textus,* 17-55,*Versio*, 12-39. See also Ch. Burchard, "Der jüdische Asenethroman," 574-81.
[2] For *Joseph and Aseneth*'s ancient names, see Ch. Burchard, *Untersuchungen,* 50-5. For its transmission history, see *id.,* "Der jüdische Asenethroman," 574-616.

Joseph will marry her. He also shows her a mysterious honeycomb and
strange-looking bees, and insists that the mysteries of the Most High
God have been revealed to her. Following this visit, Aseneth marries
Joseph—in a ceremony conducted by Pharaoh himself—and bears him
two sons, Ephraim and Manasse (cf. Gen 41:50; 46:20). Some eight years
later, when Joseph's family comes down to Egypt (cf. Gen 46:29-30),
Joseph introduces his wife to his father and brothers. The plot thickens
when Pharaoh's son, who wants Aseneth for himself, convinces four of
Joseph's brothers to help him kill Joseph and kidnap Aseneth. A battle
ensues, in which Joseph, aided by his remaining brothers, defeats the
scheming prince and his accomplices. The prince dies, Pharaoh himself
soon passes away, and Joseph retains the throne of Egypt for forty-eight
years, until Pharaoh's younger son is old enough to assume power. This
is the story's happy end.

This amusing story, which shares many traits with the Greek
novels of the Greco-Roman period, makes for very easy reading.[3] Yet in
spite of its seeming simplicity, *Joseph and Aseneth* still puzzles many
contemporary scholars who wonder, as did its sixth-century readers,
about its exact meaning. Unlike Moses, however, who was accustomed
to reading texts allegorically and decoding their edifying, Christian
meaning, modern scholars are used to a different set of interpretative
techniques. To interpret an ancient text, we often try to place it in space
and time, in the belief that only when we know who wrote it, and why,
can we decide what its original meaning and significance may have
been. Thus, there have been several attempts to locate *Joseph and
Aseneth*'s origins and to interpret its meaning, and while no attempt to
place it in one specific context has been successful, there is a broad
scholarly consensus on several important points.[4]

1) *Joseph and Aseneth* was originally written in Greek. The novel was
very popular throughout much of the Middle Ages, and has come down

---

[3] *Joseph and Aseneth*'s similarity to the Greek novels has often been noted—see,
e.g., M. Philonenko, *Joseph et Aséneth*, 43-8; Ch. Burchard, *Der dreizehnte Zeuge*,
59-86; S. West, "Joseph and Asenath," 70-81; R.I. Pervo, "Joseph and Aseneth,"
171-81.
[4] For the history of *Joseph and Aseneth* studies, see D. Sänger, *Antikes Judentum*,
11-87; Ch. Burchard, "The Present State of Research," 31-52; R.D. Chesnutt, *From
Death to Life*, 19-93. For recent challenges to the consensus outlined here, see R.S.
Kraemer, "The Book of Aseneth," 787-90; A. Standhartinger, *Das Frauenbild im
Judentum*, 14-20.

to us in numerous manuscripts in several languages. Yet there is little doubt that all these versions ultimately stem from Greek originals, and that the various Greek texts are different recensions of one *Urtext* (see further below). That *Urtext* clearly was influenced by the Greek Bible (LXX); it also used many words and concepts which do not exist in Hebrew or Aramaic. Thus, the novel is unlikely to have been translated from any Semitic original, and probably was composed in Greek.

2) *Joseph and Aseneth* is Jewish. Contrary to Moses of Aggel's *a priori* assumption that the text he was reading had a Christian message, current scholarship is almost unanimous in seeing *Joseph and Aseneth* as a Jewish work. Its protagonists are the Jewish Patriarchs, its language and style are modeled on the Hebrew Bible (in its Greek translation), and it shows no familiarity with the New Testament or with typically Christian concepts and concerns. It is, therefore, safe to assume that its author was Jewish.

3) *Joseph and Aseneth* was written in Egypt. The work deals with an Egyptian maiden and with Joseph's life in Egypt, and shows at least some familiarity with Egyptian customs and beliefs. Its Egyptian provenance is thus relatively secure.

4) *Joseph and Aseneth* was written sometime between the second century BCE and the second century CE. Since it is familiar with much of the Greek translation of the Hebrew Bible, it cannot be dated earlier than the second century BCE. If it indeed was written in Egypt, it cannot be dated later than the early second century CE, since the Jewish community of Egypt was virtually annihilated during the Jewish revolt of 115-7. These two considerations give us a general chronological time-frame within which to read *Joseph and Aseneth*.

This broad scholarly consensus, which will form the basis for the present study, already goes far beyond what a sixth-century Christian reader could (or wanted to) know about *Joseph and Aseneth*. But the scholarly quest for the origin and meaning of this work is far from over, for the claim that it was written by a Greek-speaking Egyptian Jew sometime between the second century BCE and the second century CE remains too vague to be very useful. Moreover, it is commonly agreed that "*Joseph and Aseneth* has more than its share of obscure passages," and that much in this fascinating text remains disturbingly mysterious.[5] There is, thus, no need to apologize for any attempt to reread this novel, identify its *Sitz im Leben*, and unveil some of its secrets—an attempt which forms the core of the present study.

Before reading *Joseph and Aseneth*, one must decide which text to read. The work is known in numerous Greek manuscripts, and in several ancient versions, all of which fall roughly into four textual groups, conveniently labeled *a, b, c,* and *d*.[6] Two of these, *a* and *c*, are commonly agreed to be late revisions of our novel, aimed at "improving" its Greek style. We are thus left with two text-groups, a longer recension, *b*, and a shorter, *d*, which vie for our attention. For reasons which will become apparent in the course of this study, I believe that the longer recension, *b*, is closer to the original, and it is this recension, the one championed by Ch. Burchard, which I shall analyze.[7] Unfortunately, there is no real text-critical edition of this recension, and so one must rely on Burchard's preliminary reconstruction of the Greek text, coupled with his text-critical studies and the notes which accompany his English and German translations of *Joseph and Aseneth*.[8] Burchard's text is eclectic, incorporating readings from all the Greek manuscripts and several of the ancient versions in an attempt to reconstruct a text that will be as close to the original as possible. There is, of course, no certainty that his reconstruction is correct, but I have decided to adopt his text as it stands, for in this way I hope to avoid what is probably the most common fallacy in the interpretation of ancient texts. All too often, one sees how a scholar first chooses from among the available textual witnesses those variants which best suit his understanding of the text, and then shows how well his interpretation fits the reconstructed text. By using

---

5 G.W.E. Nickelsburg, *Jewish Literature*, 261; cf. R.S. Kraemer, *Her Share*, 110.
6 Text-group *a* consists of the Greek mss. ACOPQR; *b*: Gr. mss. EFGW and the Syriac (Syr.), Armenian (Arm.), and two Latin versions (L1 and L2); *c*: Gr. mss. HJK; *d*: Gr. mss. BD and the Slavonic (Slav.) version. See Ch. Burchard, *Untersuchungen*, 2-17; id., "Zum Text," 5-9.
7 For its relation to recension *d*, see Appendix 1, below.
8 For the text, see Ch. Burchard, "Ein vorläufiger griechischer Text," 2-53, together with his *Untersuchungen*, 45-90; "Zum Text," 3-34; and "The Present State of Research," 32-5, esp. 34: "A major critical edition will therefore not be produced before long... I am thinking of republishing the preliminary text with a full apparatus... in some distant future."

Burchard's text, uninfluenced by my own interpretation of *Joseph and Aseneth*, I hope to avoid this common pitfall altogether.[9]

Finally, I would like to add a personal note. The research and writing of this book have brought me many moments of joy and fulfillment—the joy of discovery, and the fulfillment of understanding. I have tried to convey some of that joy to my readers. I am fully aware that I have thus taken upon myself a difficult task—to write a sound academic monograph which is also a pleasure to read. Whether I have succeeded is only for you, the reader, to decide.

---

[9] All translations, however, are my own, unless otherwise noted. For *Joseph and Aseneth*, I follow Burchard in providing a rather literal translation of the heavily biblicizing Greek, so as to remain faithful to the spirit as well as the meaning of the original text.

Chapter 1

Honeycomb and Bees: The Key to *Joseph and Aseneth*

Our analysis of *Joseph and Aseneth* begins with the long and elaborate scene that relates the angel's arrival, his words, and his deeds (chapters 14-7).[1] This "enigmatic episode," which baffled all previous scholars,[2] is the very heart of the novel, not only in its central position within the narrative, but in its contents as well. It is the events of this scene which pave the way for Joseph's marriage with Aseneth and all the subsequent events. Moreover, it is especially in this scene that the divine realm intervenes in an otherwise very human love story, giving *Joseph and Aseneth* its unique flavor. Thus, the lack of any coherent interpretation of this elaborate scene severely limits our understanding of the novel as a whole.

The best way to examine this scene is through a detailed and systematic reading of chapters 14 to 17, one textual unit at a time. This is a laborious, perhaps even tedious, process, but it is the only way of unfolding a complete and thorough analysis of the whole without losing sight of the smaller details.[3]

---

[1] A preliminary version of this chapter was published as G. Bohak, "Aseneth's Honeycomb and Onias' Temple."

[2] See, e.g., G. Delling, "Die Kunst des Gestaltens," 23; R.D. Chesnutt, *From Death to Life*, p. 114.

[3] In what follows I have constantly made use of the notes which accompany Ch. Burchard, "Joseph and Aseneth;" *id.*, *Joseph und Aseneth*; M. Philonenko, *Joseph et Aséneth*.

1.1. The Angel (14:1–15:2)

The scene opens with Aseneth lying on the mud-covered floor of her chamber. This arrogant maiden, who had previously refused to marry any man (2:1), saw Joseph and immediately was shattered by his beauty (6:1). Hearing that he would never even kiss an idolatrous woman (8:5-7), she locked herself up in her room and spent a whole week fasting, weeping, and praying, repenting of her arrogance and her idolatry (9:1-13:15). Tired and humiliated, she is now but a shadow of her former self. She is lying next to the window facing east (11:1y, 15, 19), waiting, it seems, for something to happen.

Suddenly, the morning star rises in the east. Aseneth sees it and rejoices, deeming that "Indeed, God has heeded my prayer, for this star rose as a messenger and herald of the light of the great day" (14:1). She keeps on looking, "and behold, next to the morning star, the heaven was torn apart (ἐσχίσθη ὁ οὐρανός) and a great and unspeakable light appeared (καὶ ἐφάνη φῶς μέγα καὶ ἀνεκλάλητον)" (14:2). Awe-struck, she falls down on her face, when suddenly a man comes out of the open heaven, approaches her, and calls her name, "Aseneth, Aseneth" (14:4). She is quite surprised that someone could enter her closed room, atop a high tower (14:5), but soon they strike up a conversation, and he introduces himself as "the chief (ἄρχων) of the house of the Lord and commander (στρατιάρχης) of all the host of the Most High" (14:8). He tells her to get up from the floor, and she lifts her head and sees him for the first time,

> a man in every respect similar to Joseph—in his robe and his crown and his royal staff. But his face was like lightning (ὡς ἀστραπή), and his eyes like sunshine (ὡς φέγγος ἡλίου), and the hairs of his head like a flame of fire of a burning torch (ὡς φλὸξ πυρὸς ὑπολαμπάδος καιομένης), and his hands and feet were like iron shining forth from a fire (ὥσπερ σίδηρος ἐκ πυρὸς ἀπολάμπων), and sparks (σπινθῆρες) shot up from his hands and feet (14:9).

To us, all this may sound like well worn clichés. The tearing open of the heaven, the appearance of great light, the angel's sudden arrival, even the fact that he calls her name twice ("Aseneth, Aseneth" in 14:4 and 14:6) are the common stock of angelic revelation scenes in ancient

Jewish literature.[4] Well-versed in the Hebrew Bible and in Jewish and Christian post-biblical literature, we would not even be impressed by the heavenly man's fiery appearance—after all, he looks like an average, run-of-the-mill angel, sparks and all.[5] Aseneth—a young Egyptian maiden—is probably unaware of these literary parallels. Yet even her instinctive reaction—falling down in utter stupefaction and keeping her face pressed to the ground—is exactly what such circumstances often demand.[6]

Seeing her reaction, the angel tries to calm her fear, and tells her to rise from the floor, go to her second room, take off her mourning garments, wash her face and hands with "living water," don a new linen robe, "untouched and exquisite," and gird herself with the double girdle of her virginity (14:12). Aseneth immediately follows his detailed instructions (14:14-5).

The meaning of this change of garments is readily apparent, for our author often uses garment-changes to signify changes in Aseneth's position and status. She began the novel in a splendid outfit, fit for the daughter of an important Egyptian priest (3:6). Yet when she heard that Joseph would never kiss an idolatrous woman she gave up her beautiful costume and donned a black mourning dress, girding a sack around her waist and sprinkling ashes on her disheveled hair (10:8-14). This change of garments was not an act of mourning (no one has died), but of supplication—when begging the Jewish God for forgiveness, she had to wear the appropriate outfit.[7] Thus, when the angel tells her to change her mourning garments for a new and pure garment, this must mean that Aseneth is a suppliant no more.

Aseneth now stands in front of the angel, who rebukes her for having covered her head with a veil, contrary to his instructions. No veil is needed, he insists, "for you are a chaste virgin today, and your head is like that of a young man (ὡς ἀνδρὸς νεανίσκου)" (15:1). Removing the veil, she is ready to hear his message.

---

[4] Torn heaven: 2 *Apoc. Bar.* 22:1; *T. Levi* 2:6; *Apoc. Abr.* 19:4, etc.—all deriving from Ezek 1:1; great light: *Apoc. Abr.* 19:4, etc.; the angel's sudden arrival: Dan 8:15; *T. Levi* 2:6; 3 *Apoc. Bar.* 1:3, etc.; calling one's name twice: 1 Sam 3:10; *Apoc. Abr.* 9:1; 20:1; Ps-Philo, *LAB* 53:3-5, etc.

[5] Dan 10:6; *Apoc. Zeph.* 7:11-2; *Apoc. Abr.* 11:2-3; 2 *Enoch* 1:4-5; Rev 2:18, etc.

[6] Dan 8:17; 1 *Enoch* 14:13-4; *Apoc. Abr.* 10:1-2, etc.

[7] Cf. Dan 9:3; Josephus, *War* II.237; *Ant.* VII.154; XIV.172-3; XX.89, 123; Ps-Philo, *LAB* 46:4; *Apoc. Mos.* 9:3. Note that Josephus describes this as a typically Jewish way of supplicating God (*Ant.* XI.231-2).

1.2. The News (15:2-16:7)

The angel now tells Aseneth the good news—that he has seen her humiliation, tears, and affliction, and that her repentance has been accepted (15:2-3). Moreover, he tells her to take courage, for he has written her name "in the book of the living in heaven (ἐν τῇ βίβλῳ τῶν ζώντων ἐν τῷ οὐρανῷ)," at its very beginning, and it will never be erased (15:4). He also promises her that

> from today, you will be renewed and refashioned and revivified, and you will eat blessed bread of life, and drink a blessed cup of immortality, and be anointed with a blessed ointment of incorruptibility (15:5).

In an earlier scene, Joseph had justified his refusal to kiss Aseneth by saying that "it does not befit a pious man, who blesses with his mouth the living God and eats blessed bread of life and drinks a blessed cup of immortality and is anointed with a blessed ointment of incorruptibility, to kiss a strange woman, who blesses with her mouth dead and dumb idols and eats from their table bread of strangulation and drinks from their libation a cup of insidiousness and is anointed with an ointment of destruction" (8:5). Moreover, at the end of that encounter he beseeched God to "bless this virgin and renew her by your spirit, and refashion her by your hidden hand, and revivify her by your life, and let her eat your bread of life and drink your cup of blessing; and count her among your people, whom you have chosen before all things came into being; and let her enter your rest, which you have prepared for your chosen ones, and live in your eternal life forever" (8:9). What we now see, then, is the angel's promise to Aseneth that Joseph's prayer will be fulfilled, and that in the future he will be free to kiss her as she desires, for the obstacles preventing such contact will have been removed.

As if that was not clear enough, the angel now reassures Aseneth that he has given her to Joseph as his eternal bride (15:6), adding that not only her status, but her name as well will undergo a striking transformation:

> And your name shall no longer be called Aseneth, but your name shall be City of Refuge (πόλις καταφυγῆς), because in you many nations will find refuge with the Lord, the Most High God, and under your wings will be sheltered many peoples who trust in the Lord God, and within your walls will be guarded those who attach themselves to the Most High God in the name of Repentance (15:7).

Following this statement is a long description of Repentance (μετανοία), who, among her other activities, "has prepared a place of rest in heaven for all those who repent" (15:7)—including, of course, Aseneth herself. Clearly, the angel envisions many other repentant persons joining Aseneth, the "City of Refuge," in that heavenly "place of rest" which Repentance has prepared for them all. It is worth noting, however, that while some of the angel's promises to Aseneth—for example, that she will marry Joseph—are fulfilled in the subsequent narrative, those promises which concern her new name, "all those who repent," and the heavenly "place of rest," remain unfulfilled to the very end. Does the angel renege on some of his promises, or will they be fulfilled at a time subsequent to the time-frame encompassed by *Joseph and Aseneth*'s narrative? For the moment, we may leave this question open and keep on reading.

Having imparted to Aseneth the joyous news, the angel now tells her that he will soon go to Joseph, "and Joseph will come to you today, and he will see you and rejoice over you, and he will love you, and he will be your husband and you will be his bride forever" (15:9). He also tells her to don her wedding robe and adorn herself with her wedding jewelry (15:10)—once again, a change of garments reflecting the change in Aseneth's status, from that of a listener to an angelic message to that of a soon-to-be bride.

Aseneth now blesses the Most High God for having sent the angel to rescue her from darkness and "from the foundations of the abyss" (15:12), and blesses the angel's own name. But what *is* his name? When she asks, he refuses to tell her, saying that his name is in heaven,

> written by the finger of God in the book of the Most High (ἐν τῇ βίβλῳ τοῦ ὑψίστου), at the beginning of the book, before all other names, for I am the chief (ἄρχων) of the house of the Most High. And all the names which are written in the book of the Most High are unspeakable, and human beings are not allowed to say them nor hear them in this world, because those names are great and wonderful and very laudable (15:12x).

This interesting statement introduces yet another heavenly book into the picture. We already know that Aseneth's name "was written in the book of the living in heaven, at the beginning of the book," by the angel's finger (15:4). Now we hear that the angel's name is written, by the finger of God, at the beginning of "the book of the Most High." These seem to be two different books, for his name and hers cannot both occupy the first line in the same book, and, in any case, the names in the second book, "the book of the Most High," are said to be "unspeakable (ἄρρητα)," which Aseneth's name certainly is not. It seems, therefore, that one book, "the book of the living," is for righteous human beings, and is kept by the angel, and the other, "the book of the Most High," is for angels, and is kept by God himself. Unfortunately, the angel does not elaborate on this issue any further.

As for his insistence on keeping his name a secret, many scholars have refused to grant him his wish, and assumed that the author must have the archangel Michael in mind.[8] This is, in my view, an imprudent interpretative move. Not only must we let angels have things their way, and keep their name secret if they so wish (especially in light of such biblical precedents as Gen 32:28-9 and Judg 13:17-8), we must also avoid reading into the text names and ideas which appear in other strands of post-biblical Jewish literature and belief, and which may be irrelevant, or even misleading, for the study of *Joseph and Aseneth*.

The angel's refusal to divulge his name sounds like a real conversation-stopper. Had the author so wished, the story could have moved directly to chapter 18, to Joseph's arrival and the subsequent wedding, the natural consequence of the angel's visit. But this is not the case. Instead of bidding the messenger farewell and going on with the story, Aseneth suddenly invites him to lunch. Instead of politely refusing and taking his leave, he agrees—and comes up with an unusual request: "Bring me also a honeycomb" (16:1). Aseneth is quite distressed by this unexpected wish, since she does not have a honeycomb. She offers to send a slave boy to get one, but he says that she should find one in her storeroom (16:5). She insists that there is no honeycomb there, but he is just as persistent, and she gives up and goes to the other room (16:6-7).

1.3. The Honeycomb (16:8-16x)

> And Aseneth went into her storeroom and found a honeycomb lying on the table. And the comb was big and white as snow and full of honey. And that honey was like dew from heaven and its breath like a breath of life. And Aseneth was amazed, and said to herself,

---

[8] E.g., V. Aptowitzer, "Asenath," 276; G.D. Kilpatrick, "The Last Supper," 5; J. Jeremias, "The Last Supper," 91; G.W.E. Nickelsburg, *Jewish Literature*, 259; R. Doran, "Narrative Literature," 292.

Surely, this comb came out of this man's mouth, for its breath is like the breath of this man's mouth (16:8-9).

She brings the honeycomb to the angel, who sarcastically reminds her how she had insisted that she did not have a honeycomb (16:10). She is afraid, and says once again that she did not have one, "but you spoke and it came into being. Did this comb come out of your mouth—for its breath is like the breath of your mouth?" (16:11). He smiles at Aseneth's understanding, and pats her head with his right hand (16:12-3). She is terrified by his spark-emitting hand, and he smiles again and says to her:

> Blessed are you, Aseneth, because the unspeakable mysteries of the Most High were revealed to you (ἀπεκαλύφθη σοι τὰ ἀπόρρητα μυστήρια τοῦ ὑψίστου), and blessed are all those who attach themselves to the Lord God in repentance (οἱ προσκείμενοι τῷ θεῷ τῷ ὑψίστῳ ἐν ὀνόματι τῆς μετανοίας), because they will eat from this comb. For this comb is a spirit of life. And the bees of Paradise have made it from the dew of the roses of life in God's Paradise. And all the angels of God (οἱ ἄγγελοι τοῦ θεοῦ) eat from it and all the chosen ones of God (οἱ ἐκλεκτοὶ τοῦ θεοῦ) and all the sons of the Most High (οἱ υἱοὶ τοῦ ὑψίστου), because it is a comb of life, and whoever eats from it will not die forever (16:14).

Something very important seems to have happened here, just when we might have expected the scene to be drawing to a close. A mysterious honeycomb suddenly appeared in our scene, a comb made in heaven and consumed by the angels, by "the chosen ones of God," and by "the sons of the Most High." We already know that Joseph is "the (firstborn) son of God" (6:3, 5; 13:13; 18:11; 21:4; 23:10). We also remember that in his prayer Joseph beseeched God to "count Aseneth among your people, whom you have chosen (τῷ λαῷ σου ὃν ἐξελέξω) before all things came into being," and let her go to the "place of rest" which God has prepared "for (his) chosen ones (τοῖς ἐκλεκτοῖς σου)" (8:9). But the identity of these "sons of God" and of the "chosen ones" is never specified, and the statement that "the unspeakable mysteries of the Most High were revealed" to Aseneth—which sounds suspiciously familiar to readers of post-biblical Jewish and Christian literature[9]— also goes unexplained.

> And the man stretched out his right hand and broke a small part off the comb, and he ate (some of it), and what was left he threw with

[9] 3 Enoch 11:1-2; T. Levi 2:10; 18:2; 3 Apoc. Bar. 1:6, 8; 2:6; etc.

his hand into Aseneth's mouth, and said to her, "Eat." And she ate. And the man said to Aseneth, "Behold, you ate bread of life, and drank a cup of immortality, and were anointed with an ointment of incorruptibility. Behold, from today your flesh will bloom like flowers of life from the land of the Most High, and your bones will grow like the cedars of God's Paradise, and untiring powers will embrace you, and your youth will not see old age, and your beauty will not diminish forever. And you shall be like a walled mother-city of all those who seek refuge in the name of the Lord God, the king of the ages" (16:15-6).

The story is getting more complicated, so we must pay close attention to even its smallest details. The angel eats from the honeycomb, an action which is in line with his previous statement that "all the angels of God eat from it" (16:14). Aseneth too eats from the same honeycomb, which probably means that she is now one of "the chosen ones of God" and "the sons of the Most High" who were also said to share this comb (16:14). Thus, one element of Joseph's prayer (8:9) has been fulfilled, for Aseneth now indeed is counted among "the chosen ones of God." Moreover, the angel's claim that Aseneth has eaten "bread of life," drunk "a cup of immortality," and been anointed with "an ointment of incorruptibility," fulfills another of Joseph's wishes—although Joseph himself made no mention of anointing (8:9). It also fits well with the angel's own promise to Aseneth just a short while earlier (16:5). Finally, since the food-drink-ointment sequence is somehow typical of Joseph himself, and Joseph is "the (firstborn) son of God," Aseneth's participation in the same sequence further implies that she has joined "the chosen ones of God" and "the sons of the Most High," an inclusion which assures her supernatural strength and beauty, accompanied by immortal youth.[10] Once again, however, we must note that at least one of the angel's promises—that Aseneth will be "like a walled mother-city of all those who seek refuge in the name of the Lord God"—remains unfulfilled to the very end of the story.

1.4. The Bees (16:17-23)

Going back to Aseneth and her visitor, we find him touching the broken comb and restoring it to its previous shape (16:16x). He then traces two lines across the comb, dividing it—like a loaf of bread— into four equal

---

[10] Cf. the descriptions of Aseneth's subsequent beauty in 18:9-11 and 21:4.

parts, "and the way of his finger became like blood" (16:17).[11] Yet even this cosmetic surgery is not the end of the angel's visit, for we now come to the most enigmatic part of the honeycomb scene, and of *Joseph and Aseneth* as a whole:

> And the man said to the comb, "Come." And bees rose from the cells of the comb, and the cells were innumerable, myriads upon myriads and thousands upon thousands (μυριάδες μυριάδων καὶ χιλιάδες χιλιάδων). And the bees were white as snow (λευκαὶ ὡσεὶ χιών), and their wings were like purple and like violet and like scarlet and like gold-woven linen garments (καὶ τὰ πτερὰ αὐτῶν ὡς πορφύρα καὶ ὡς ὑάκινθος καὶ ὡς κόκκος καὶ ὡς βύσσινα ἱμάτια χρυσοϋφῆ), and they had golden diadems (διαδήματα χρυσᾶ) on their heads, and they had sharp stings, but they harmed no one. And all these bees encircled Aseneth from her feet to her head. And other bees were large and chosen like their queens, and they rose from the damaged part[12] of the comb and encircled Aseneth's face, and made upon her mouth and her lips a comb similar to the comb which was lying before the man (κηρίου ὅμοιον τῷ κηρίῳ τῷ παρακειμένῳ τῷ ἀνθρώπῳ). And all these bees ate from the comb which was on Aseneth's mouth. (16:17x-20).

What is going on here, and who are these strange-looking bees buzzing through Aseneth's room? Clearly, these cannot be actual bees, for nature has yet to see such multicolored bees with "golden diadems on their heads," and nowhere in ancient literature do we find any bees even remotely similar to what we have here. Thus, we are tempted to think that the exotic bees might have some symbolic significance within the narrative. But what do they signify?

The first clue to the bees' identity is their behavior, which corresponds well with Greco-Roman apiological lore. Ancient observers were not unaware of bees' swarming habits, and often compared their tendency to leave their comb and settle elsewhere to similar types of human behavior. As a typical example of this political analogy we may quote Philo's description of how "when the swarm (of bees) thrives and their numbers increase, as when a city gets overpopulated, they migrate

---

[11] For marking bread and cakes with cross-cuts at right angles, see, e.g., Hesiod, *Op.* 442; Virgil, *Aeneid* VII.115; *Moretum* 47-9 ("iamque subactum (i.e., the dough)... dilatat in orbem / et notat impressis aequo discrimine quadris").

[12] "From the damaged part (ἀπὸ τῆς πληγῆς)" is Burchard's tentative suggestion. "From the tablet (of the honeycomb) (ἀπὸ τῆς πλακός)" is also possible. See Ch. Burchard, "Ein vorläufiger griechischer Text," 50, n. 18, and below, n. 27.

to another place, setting out, as it were, to establish a colony."[13] Thus, one possible explanation of the bees' behavior here is that they leave their old home behind and establish a new colony on Aseneth's mouth, an action parallel to the establishment of a new human colony in a distant land.

A second possible clue has to do with the location of the new honeycomb, namely, Aseneth's mouth. There is, of course, no parallel in the natural world to such an action, but ancient literature does provide ample parallels here. Quite a few people—including Homer, Pindar, Sophocles, Plato, and Ambrose, to name but a few—were said to have shared this experience of having a swarm of bees alight on their lips and deposit their honey or wax there.[14] In all these cases, however, the bees' landing on a person's lips portended his future rhetorical or poetical achievements, which would seem quite irrelevant in Aseneth's case. In fact, it is only with Joseph's kisses that she receives "a spirit of wisdom," and "a spirit of truth" (19:11), and even then she does not seem to possess any conspicuous rhetorical abilities. Thus, the erection of the new honeycomb specifically on Aseneth's mouth probably is unrelated to similar scenes in Greco-Roman literature. In fact, it would seem more likely that Aseneth's mouth was chosen as the site for the bees' building activity in order to purify it from its defiled state (11:9, 16; 12:5), so that Joseph would be able to kiss it (19:11)—which he had previously refused to do (8:5).

A third clue to the scene relates to the bees' appearance. While the angel was said to be "a man in every respect similar to Joseph, in his robe and his crown and his royal staff" (14:9), the bees too seem to share this resemblance, with their golden diadems, their multicolored "garments," and perhaps even their sharp stings, suitable substitutes for the angel's, and Joseph's, royal staffs. We may also note that the bees who build the new honeycomb on Aseneth's lips eat from the new comb—they are doing the very same thing which Aseneth herself did several verses earlier (16:15), after she was told that all the angels of God, the "chosen ones of God," and the "sons of the Most High," eat from it (16:14). Since the bees who build the new honeycomb and eat

---

[13] Philo, *De Animal.* 65 (tr. Terian, 96). See also Plato, *Politicus* 293d; Xenophon, *Oeconomicus* VII.34; Varro, *RR* III.16.29-31; Aelian, *NA* V.13.

[14] Olck, "Biene," 447-8. Two close parallels to our scene are Aelian, *VH* XII.45 (bees built a honeycomb on Plato's mouth), and Pausanias, IX.23.2 (bees plastered Pindar's lips with wax).

from it are also said to be "chosen (ἐκλεκταί)," there is no doubt that they somehow belong with the angel, Joseph, Aseneth, and their kind.

But the fourth, and most important, clue to the bees' identity lies in a closer examination of their appearance. They are said to be "white as snow, and their wings like purple and like violet and like scarlet and like gold-woven linen garments." This combination of four weaving materials—purple (πορφύρα), violet (ὑάκινθος), scarlet (κόκκος) and linen (βύσσος)[15]—is a most telling clue, for it is out of these four materials that many objects in the Jewish temple, including the priestly garments, were made. One relevant biblical passage is Exod 28:4-5:

> They (the craftsmen) shall make sacred vestments for Aaron your brother and his sons to wear when they serve me as my priests, using gold, violet (LXX: ὑάκινθος), purple (πορφύρα), scarlet (κόκκινον), and linen (βύσσος).

There are, of course, many more biblical passages in which these four materials, often coupled with gold, are used for the various weaving projects connected with the desert tabernacle, the Jerusalem temple(s), and the priestly regalia.[16] Moreover, numerous passages in post-biblical Jewish and Christian literature deal with this fourfold combination of materials, demonstrating its priestly connotation for any reader of the Greek Bible.[17] In fact, the only passages in ancient Greek literature—Jewish, Christian, and "pagan"—in which this combination of four materials may be found are passages that deal with the Jewish temple and the Jewish priesthood.[18] Thus, it is safe to assume that the mention of the four materials in our scene must point to a Jewish priestly setting, and the bees, with their diadems and priestly "garments," must be a symbolic representation of Jewish priests. This could also explain their apparent similarity to the angel himself, in their garments and diadems,

---

[15] Here and elsewhere, I translate βύσσος as "linen," in line with common scholarly usage, but cf. S. Dally, "Ancient Assyrian Textiles," 121, for a detailed discussion of its real nature. I am grateful to Stephanie West for this reference.
[16] E.g., Exod 25:3; 26:1, 31, 36; 27:16; 28:5, 8, 15; 35:6, 25 etc. L.M. Wills, The Jewish Novel, 174 n. 36, refers to an unpublished paper by Cynthia Baker that apparently makes a similar point.
[17] E.g., Philo, Vita Mosis II.88; Cong. 117 etc.; Josephus, War V.213 etc.; Protev. Iacobi X.1; Clem. Alex., Strom. V.6; Epiphanius, Panar., XXXIV.16; Irenaeus, Adv. Haer. I.18.2; Greg. Nyss., De vita Mosis, 196 etc.
[18] This statement is based on an Ibycus search of the TLG CD ROM #D. The one possible exception is LXX Isa 3:21-4, where we find τὰ βύσσινα, τὰ ὑακίνθινα, τὰ κόκκινα, τὰ περιπόρφυρα and τὰ μεσοπόρφυρα mentioned as luxury items.

for the similarity between priests and angels is a common motif of ancient Jewish literature.[19]

If the bees stand for Jewish priests, the honeycomb they live in certainly must stand for their temple. After all, it is in a temple that we would expect to see "myriads upon myriads and thousands upon thousands" of cells with priests, especially since this very phrase is commonly used in Jewish and early Christian literature to describe the ministering angels in the heavenly temple.[20] Moreover, the association of a honeycomb with a temple has much to recommend it, given the structural similarities between bee-hives and temples—both depend on the perfect orchestration of numerous attendants' minutely conceived individual tasks, and both are headed by one supreme ruler. Moreover, both bees and priests share a strong emphasis on purity and chastity.[21] This association often occurred elsewhere in the ancient world, as in Delphi, for example, where the Pythia was known as μέλισσα, "bee," and local tradition—as reported by Pausanias—claimed that Apollo's second-most ancient temple "was made by bees from beeswax and feathers."[22]

Whether the author was aware of such antecedents to his symbolic use of the honeycomb we may never know, for he easily could have developed it himself. What is more important, however, is that once the bees' significance is understood, the scene may be read not only on its surface level—a swarm of bees leaving its comb to establish a new one—but on its symbolic level as well. What the bees are doing when they leave the original honeycomb and build a new comb, similar to the old one, on Aseneth's lips and mouth, could mean only one thing. It must

---

19 E.g., *T. Levi* 3:5-6; *Jub.* 30:18; 31:14; Philo, *Spec. Leg.* I.66, and M. Himmelfarb, *Ascent to Heaven*, 18-22, 29-46.

20 Dan 7:10: "Thousands upon thousands served him, and myriads upon myriads attended his presence." *1 Enoch* 40:1; 60:1; 71:8; *Apoc. Zeph.* 4:2; 8:2; Rev 5:11; etc.

21 For bees' proverbial purity and chastity, see Aristotle, *HA* VIII(IX).626a.24-25 (καθαριώτατόν ἐστι τὸ ζῷον); Varro, *RR* III.16.6; Pliny, *NH* XI.16.44; Aelian, *NA* I.10, and G. Robert-Turnow, *De Apium Mellisque*, 12-18. For the importance of chastity in Jewish priestly circles, see Schürer (rev.), *History*, 2:240-2.

22 For the bee-priest(ess) metaphor, see Olck, "Biene," 448; L. Bodson, *IEPA ZΩIA*, 25-43. For Delphi, see esp. Pindar, *Pyth.* IV.60; Pausanias, X.5.9: λέγουσι οἱ Δελφοὶ γενέσθαι ὑπὸ μελισσῶν τὸν ναὸν ἀπό τε τοῦ κηροῦ τῶν μελισσῶν καὶ ἐκ πτερῶν. (cf. Philostratus, *Vita Apollonii* VI.10). I owe this reference to Ernst Bammel, who, setting out from this source, independently arrived at an interpretation of the honey-comb scene similar to the one proposed here.

be an attempt to show Aseneth how some Jewish priests leave their own temple and build a new one, similar to the one they had left behind.

Suddenly, we can be very specific: the description of Jewish priests leaving their temple and building a second temple could, of course, refer to one of several known historical episodes—the establishment of the Elephantine temple in the sixth century BCE, of the Samaritan temple in the fourth century (or later), or of Onias' temple in the second century BCE—or to another, less-known event.[23] But the fact that the new honeycomb-temple is built in Aseneth's room, in Heliopolis, leaves little room for doubt—the symbolic vision must refer to the establishment of Onias' temple in Heliopolis in the second century BCE, a temple modeled after the one in Jerusalem (see below, Chapter 2.1.4). In such a case, the bloody incisions in the honeycomb which precede the bees' departure (16:17) probably refer to the priestly feuds of the 170s and 160s BCE, and perhaps even to Antiochus' desecration of the Jerusalem temple in 167 BCE—events that directly preceded Onias' flight to Egypt and the establishment of his Heliopolitan temple (below, Chapter 2.1.1).

There is, however, much more that the angel seems to be showing Aseneth, for the symbolic revelation is not over yet:

> And the man said to the bees, "Go to your place." And all the bees rose and flew and went off into heaven. And those who wished to harm Aseneth fell on the ground and died. And the man stretched out his staff over the dead bees and said to them, "Rise you, too, and go off to your place." And the dead bees rose and went off into the court adjoining Aseneth's house and settled on the fruit-bearing trees (16:20-3).

It is, of course, hardly surprising that when the angel sends the bees to "their place" they all go straight to heaven—this is exactly what he meant when he said that whoever eats from the honeycomb "will not die forever" (16:14), and when he told Aseneth, once she ate a bit, that her youth "will not see old age" (16:16). The bees must have gone to God's Paradise, whence they seem to have come (cf. 16:14), or to that "place of rest in heaven" which God and Repentance have prepared for all the "chosen ones" (8:9; cf. 15:7; 22:13), to live there forever. What *is* surprising, however, is that we now learn that whereas the bees who

---

23 For the Elephantine temple, see B. Porten, *Archives from Elephantine*, 119-22; for the Samaritan temple, e.g., M. Mor, "Samaritan history," 4-10; H. Eshel, "The Prayer of Joseph," 129-34. See also E.F. Campbell, "Jewish Shrines."

built the honeycomb on Aseneth's mouth "had sharp stings, but they
harmed no one (οὐκ ἠδίκουν τινά)" (16:18), there are other bees too, bad
bees which suddenly appear, as if from nowhere, and try to injure
Aseneth (ὅσαι ἠβουλήθησαν ἀδικῆσαι τὴν Ἀσενέθ). Once again, this
event may be interpreted on two levels. On the surface level, we are
dealing with another well known natural phenomenon, and a common
topos of ancient literature, namely, the division of bees into building-
bees on the one hand and robber-bees and drones on the other, and the
constant strife between these groups. Like the bees' swarming, this
phenomenon too was often used metaphorically to describe social
tensions, and civil wars, among humans.[24] On the symbolic level,
however, we cannot help seeing here a reference to some Jewish priests
who tried to harm Onias' project after his flight to Egypt. One would
love to know who exactly these wicked priests were, and what it was
that they tried to do, but the paucity of the available evidence—and
Josephus' silence on this score—preclude any clear identification.[25]

While the bad bees' exact identity remains unknown, the angel's
benevolence toward them certainly deserves a comment. When they fall
dead, he does not do away with them altogether, but raises them back to
life and lets them settle in Aseneth's courtyard. On the narrative's
surface level, there may be yet another bit of ancient apiological lore
here, namely, the notion that dead bees can be brought back to life, if
only the right measures are taken.[26] On the symbolic level, however, the
angel's action must mean that once the wicked priests' attempt to harm
Onias' project fails, the priests themselves must be forgiven and given a
second chance. Naturally, they do not go to heaven, to join the good
bees and the "chosen ones of God," but at least they are allowed to stay
in Aseneth's courtyard with its fruit-bearing trees. Presumably, they too
might go to heaven one day, to that "place of rest" which God and
Repentance have prepared for all those who repent (15:7)—provided, of
course, that they do repent and their repentance is accepted. Clearly, the
insistence on forgiving one's enemies—a recurrent theme throughout
Joseph and Aseneth (cf. below, Chapter 3.3-4)—is directly related to the
glowing description of Repentance, God's lovely daughter (15:7).

---

[24] See Philo, *De Animal.* 61 (tr. Terian, 95) and the numerous examples cited by
Olck, "Biene," 433, 437.
[25] The Talmudic legend says of Onias that "his brethren the priests sought to kill
him" (b *Menahot* 109b)—but one hesitates to lean on such a broken reed.
[26] Columella, *RR* IX.13.3-4; Pliny, *NH* XI.22.69.

1.5. The Vision Ends (17:1-10)

The scene is drawing to a close, but several issues have yet to be settled. First, the angel asks Aseneth whether she has seen it all, and then promises her, "So will be (οὕτως ἔσται) all my words which I have spoken to you today" (17:2). Having shown her the events of the distant future, he now insists that the vision, and all his promises, will be fulfilled just as foretold. His next action, however, is more intriguing:

> And the man stretched out his right hand for the third time, and touched the damaged part[27] of the comb, and fire immediately went up from the table and consumed the comb, but did not harm the table. And much fragrance came forth from the burning of the comb and filled the room (17:3-4).

Why is the angel burning the honeycomb? A casual reading might give us the impression that once the honeycomb vision is over, the angel has to get rid of the honeycomb itself. This cannot be the right answer, however, for we must note (a) that clean-up time comes later, when the angel tells Aseneth to put the table away, at the very end of the scene (17:7), and (b) that *only one honeycomb is consumed by the fire.* If the angel wanted to tidy up Aseneth's room and rid it of any incriminating evidence, why not have the fire consume the second honeycomb too, the one built by the swarming bees on Aseneth's lips and mouth?

There is, of course, a second possibility, namely, that the symbolic vision is not over yet, and the burning of the honeycomb is itself a part of that vision. If this is so, it would seem that having shown Aseneth how some priests would leave the Jerusalem temple and build a new one, similar to the first, the angel also shows her how the original temple would be consumed by a great fire and only the second temple, the one in Heliopolis, would remain. Naturally, this interpretation could influence not only our understanding of the entire scene, but the date we would assign it as well. This is, however, an issue which is best left open for the time being, for only after a detailed analysis of the history of Onias' temple can this question be approached in a more meaningful manner (below, Chapter 5.3).

---

[27] "The damaged part (τῆς πληγῆς)" AP Syr. Arm.—see Ch. Burchard, "Joseph and Aseneth," 230. n. 6.

The original honeycomb gone, Aseneth now asks the angel to bless her seven virgin maidens, "just as you blessed me" (17:4). She calls them to her room,

> and the man blessed them and said, "The Lord the Most High God will bless you, and you shall be seven pillars of the City of Refuge, and all those (fem.) who join the chosen ones of that city (αἱ σύνοικοι τῶν ἐκλεκτῶν τῆς πόλεως ἐκείνης) will rest upon you forever" (17:6).

What happens here is an interesting twist to Aseneth's transformation. The seven pillars clearly point to Prov 9:1, "Wisdom has built her house, she has hewn her seven pillars."[28] Thus, Aseneth is destined to become not only a "City of Refuge," but a house of wisdom as well, in which "the chosen ones," and all those who join them, will live forever. We must note, however, that this is yet another angelic promise which goes unfulfilled in *Joseph and Aseneth*'s narrative.

His mission accomplished, the angel is ready to leave. He tells Aseneth to put the table away (17:7), and when she turns around he quickly disappears.

> And Aseneth saw something like a four-horse chariot, going into heaven toward the east. And the chariot was like a flame of fire, and the horses like lightning. And the man was standing on that chariot (17:8).

Flying away in his fiery chariot, so similar to Joseph's (5:4, and cf. 14:9), the angel vanishes into heaven, and Aseneth is awe-struck once again. Afraid that she may have said something inappropriate—"I said that a man came from heaven into my room, and I did not know that a god came to me" (17:9)—she begs him to be gracious to her and forgive her for speaking boldly in his presence (ἵλεως ἔσο... διότι ἐγὼ λελάληκα τολμηρῶς ἐνώπιόν σου, 17:10). But "while Aseneth was still saying these things to herself, a young man from Pentephres' retinue rushed in" (18:1), and the romantic plot rolls on in full force. The honeycomb scene over, Aseneth must prepare herself for Joseph's visit and the longed-for wedding. We, however, must leave her there, and revert to our own quest for the date, provenance, and meaning of *Joseph and Aseneth*, for

---

28 Note, however, that the word used for pillars (κίονες) is different from the word used in LXX Prov 9:1 (στύλοι).

the close analysis of the honeycomb scene has lead to several surprising discoveries.

1) The honeycomb scene is not, as some scholars have suggested, a conversion scene—in fact, Aseneth's conversion is already complete, and approved, at its very beginning (15:2-10)[29]—but an apocalyptic-revelation scene, one of many scenes in ancient Jewish and Christian literature in which an angel teaches a biblical hero(ine) the hidden mysteries that most human beings are not supposed to know. This would account for many of the scene's constituent motifs, from the torn heavens, the great light, and the sudden appearance of a fiery angel, through his insistence that "the unspeakable mysteries of the Most High were revealed" to Aseneth, to the symbolic scenario which he enacts in her room.[30]

2) If angelic revelation-scenes may roughly be divided into those that focus on the mysteries of nature and those that focus on future events, our scene clearly belongs with the second, "historical," type. This would account for the recurrent use of the future tense throughout the scene, which stands in marked contrast to the past tense used in other sections of *Joseph and Aseneth*.[31] It would also account for the fact that some of the angel's promises to Aseneth go unfulfilled—clearly, they were meant to be fulfilled in the author's own time—and for the eschatological overtones of the entire scene, a subject to which we shall return in Chapter 5.

3) Our final, and most important discovery, is that what the angel was showing Aseneth in the symbolic vision was how a group of Jewish priests would leave the Jerusalem temple one day and build a second temple, similar to the first, in Heliopolis. In other words, he was describing to her the establishment of Onias' temple in the second century BCE. There is, of course, no sign that Aseneth herself understood the real meaning of what she has been shown; indeed, her subsequent conversations with Joseph (19:5-6), and with her steward (18:10-1) clearly imply that she did not—at least until Levi reveals it to

---

[29] D. Sänger, *Antikes Judentum*, 156-7; R.D. Chesnutt, *From Death to Life*, 124-5.
[30] For a correct identification of the honeycomb scene's literary genre, see now E. Humphrey, *The Ladies and the Cities*, 35-39.
[31] "You will" (15:4, 7; 16:16, etc.), "they will" (15:7; 16:16; 18:6, etc.), etc.

her in secret (22:13).[32] But as long as the intended readers of *Joseph and Aseneth* could understand the symbolic vision, there was no need, from the author's point of view, to make the protagonist herself comprehend what she sees. She could serve as an excellent medium, even if she entirely missed the message.

These three discoveries lead to a more general conclusion, namely, that the honeycomb scene, and, presumably, *Joseph and Aseneth* as a whole, were written by someone who was closely associated with Onias' temple. This provides us with a possible provenance for *Joseph and Aseneth*, and a new vantage point from which to reexamine the entire novel. To make full use of that vantage point, however, we must first put our novel aside and turn to the historical episode symbolically depicted in our scene. Elucidating the establishment of Onias' temple, and its subsequent history, could help us in our quest not only for the origins of *Joseph and Aseneth*, but for its purpose and meaning as well.

---

[32] Aseneth, who had previously poked fun at Joseph for having interpreted Pharaoh's dreams, "just like the older women of the Egyptians" (4:10), displays a remarkable lack of interpretative acumen herself.

Chapter 2

A Brief History of Onias' Temple

The history of Onias' temple is a relatively obscure one. Josephus, our main source, provides two different accounts of its establishment, and briefly mentions several later events connected with the Oniad Jews and their temple. Eusebius and Jerome supply a few details not found in Josephus, but never devote much space to this distant episode. Rabbinic literature preserves an account of the temple's foundation that is so fantastic, and displays such gross errors, as to be of little historical value. Apart from these sources and those dependent on them, only small bits of evidence are available: some biblical verses in Hebrew, Greek, and Aramaic, an obscure passage of the Fifth Sibylline Oracle, a few dozen tombstones, and some badly mutilated papyri. Setting out from these meager sources, we divide our study into three sections, one devoted to the establishment of Onias' temple, another to its subsequent history, and a third section dealing with its final destruction.[1]

2.1. The Establishment of Onias' Temple

The thirty five years from 175 to 140 BCE were one of the most tumultuous periods of Jewish history. Within this short period, several

---

[1] The secondary literature on Onias' temple—beginning with Cassel's *Dissertatio* (1730)—is enormous; it also abounds in false starts and questionable assumptions (cf. below, Chapter 7). In what follows, no attempt has been made to provide a full survey of that literature.

major events—the bloody feuds within the Jewish priestly class, the desecration of the Jerusalem temple by Antiochus IV, the Maccabean revolt, and the emergence of an independent Jewish state—dramatically changed the future course of the Jewish people as a whole. These events, and the transfer of power from the old high priestly line of the sons of Zadok to a previously unknown priestly family, the Hasmoneans, are too well known to be discussed here at great detail.[2] What we must focus on is just one by-product of these grand developments, namely, the establishment of Onias' temple in Heliopolis, Egypt.

2.1.1. When Was It Built?

When Onias III was treacherously murdered in Antioch, ca. 171 BCE,[3] he left behind a son, Onias IV, who must have been quite young at the time.[4] This Onias eventually made his way to Egypt, with a large group of followers,[5] and permanently settled there.

The precise date of this move is a notoriously vexed question. Both 1 and 2 Maccabees, as well as the Book of Daniel, never mention Onias' flight to Egypt and the establishment of his temple there. Josephus, on the other hand, provides us with two different accounts of this event. In the *War*, where he erroneously assumed Onias' temple to have been founded by Onias III, he placed Onias' flight immediately following Antiochus' desecration of the Jerusalem temple, i.e., in 166 BCE. In the *Antiquities*, however, where he already knows that Onias' temple was founded by Onias IV, but still errs in some details, Josephus claims that

---

2 See, e.g., E. Bickerman, *The God of the Maccabees*; V. Tcherikover, *Hellenistic Civilization*, 117-265; M. Hengel, *Judaism and Hellenism*, 1:267-309; Schürer (rev.), *History*, 1:137-99.

3 2 Macc 4:34. Dan 9:26; 11:22 and 1 Enoch 90:8 probably refer to this event—cf. J.A. Montgomery, *A Critical Commentary*, 381-2, 451; J.J. Collins, *Daniel*, 356, 382; P.A. Tiller, *A Commentary*, 352-4. The various scholarly attempts to deny Onias III's murder and attribute to him the establishment of Onias' temple were refuted by M. Stern, "The Death of Onias III." More recent attempts, such as V. Keil, "Onias III," and F. Parente, "Onias III's Death," fail to adduce any new evidence.

4 Josephus, *Ant.* XII.237, 387, perhaps supported by Dan 9:26. Since Onias' two sons were still serving as military commanders in 103 BCE (see below), Josephus' statements seem reliable.

5 *Ant.* XIII.73; Cf. Jerome, *In Dan.* III.XI.14 (ed. Glorie, 908-9): "Onias sacerdos, assumptis Iudaeorum plurimis, fugit in Aegypto... sub occasione igitur Oniae pontificis, infinita examina Iudaeorum Aegyptum confugerunt."

2. A Brief History of Onias' Temple

Onias left Jerusalem only after the high priesthood was conferred upon Iakimos-Alcimus, i.e., in 162 BCE.[6] How are we to decide which of these accounts is correct, and reconstruct the events of Onias' escape? Judging from the fantastic scenarios proposed in the past,[7] it probably would be wiser not to attempt such a reconstruction at all, especially since our main piece of evidence is of a very dubious nature. This is a letter of 21 September 164 BCE, sent by the διοικητής Herodes to a high-ranking official whose name is badly mutilated. Wilcken's reconstruction of the original name as 'Ονίᾳ ("to Onias"), accepted by most subsequent scholars, could imply that Onias IV was the addressee of this letter, thus providing a *terminus ad quem*, September 164, for his arrival in Egypt.[8] Yet Wilcken's reading—ingenious as it is—remains doubtful, and cannot serve as a sound basis on which to build complex historical hypotheses.[9] Thus, we are left with possibilities rather than certainties—Onias may have fled to Egypt either immediately following his father's assassination, or at the time of Antiochus' persecution, which led to a large exodus of Jews from Jerusalem (1 Macc 1:38), or in 162 BCE, when Alcimus' nomination to the high priesthood dashed his own hopes of attaining that position. Without further evidence, any attempt to be more specific would be no more than vain speculation.

As for Onias' Heliopolitan temple, and the date of its construction, we have no reliable evidence whatsoever. In fact, the only available data are Josephus' claim that Onias' temple stood for 343 years, and Jerome's claim that it stood for 250 years.[10] Since the temple was destroyed ca. 74 CE (see below), neither figure is acceptable. Josephus' 343 might be some symbolic number—the equivalent of seven Jubilees (7x7x7)[11]—or a copyist's error, in which case we may wish to emend it to 243. Even this emendation, however, does not solve the problem, since it would place the erection of Onias' temple ca. 169/8 BCE, which is too early. Jerome's figure of 250 is even less plausible, and so we are left

---

6 *War* I.31-3; VII.423; *Ant.* XII.387; XX.235-6.
7 E.g., M.A. Beek, "Relations," 121-32; J.G. Bunge, "Zur Geschichte," 1-46.
8 CPJ I, 132=UPZ 110. For Wilcken's own interpretation, see UPZ, 487-8. Cf. V. Tcherikover's note on CPJ I, 132; M. Delcor, "Le temple d'Onias," 192-3; J. Mélèze Modrzejewski, *Les juifs d'Egypte*, 103-5.
9 See E.S. Gruen, "Origins and Objectives."
10 Josephus, *War* VII.436; Jerome, *In Dan.* III.XI.14.
11 See, e.g., Thackery, LCL *Josephus*, 3:627; R. Hayward, "The Jewish Temple," 434-7; J. Mélèze Modrzejewski, *Les juifs d'Egypte*, 107-8.

with no firm basis for dating the erection of Onias' temple, beyond the obvious suggestion that it occurred after Ptolemy VI Philometor's return from Rome, in Summer 163, and before his death in Syria, in 145 BCE.[12]

2.1.2. Why Heliopolis?

Onias' choice of Egypt as a safe haven is hardly surprising. Ptolemaic Egypt was the Seleucids' traditional foe, and an enemy of one's enemy is bound to be one's friend. It is also likely that Onias and his followers had been pro-Ptolemaic all along, and that it was in part for fear of Seleucid reprisals that they chose to leave Jerusalem.[13] Moreover, many Jews already were well established throughout Egypt, so Onias' supporters could look for help from their Egyptian brethren.[14]

When they came to Egypt, they asked its rulers' permission to settle in Heliopolis, so that—and all our sources are unanimous on this point[15]—they might fulfill Isaiah's ancient prophecy:

> In that day there shall be five cities in the land of Egypt speaking the language of Canaan and swearing to the Lord of Hosts; one of them shall be called the City of the Sun (עיר החרס).[16] In that day there shall be an altar (מזבח) to the Lord in the land of Egypt, and a pillar (מצבה) for the Lord upon her frontier (Isa 19:18-9).

This is not the place to discuss what Isaiah, or his interpolators, might have meant in this prophecy, but it should be stressed that the suggestion that these verses are an Oniad *vaticinium ex eventu* has long been put to rest, with the discovery of the Qumran Isaiah Scroll (1QIs^a) which already contains this passage.[17] Onias and his followers—living in an age which scrutinized the Prophets' promises and compared them with current events—must have paid especially close attention to this

---

12 For the date of Philometor's return to Egypt in 163 BCE, see E. Lanciers, "Die Alleinherrschaft," 407-10.
13 See *War* I.32; *Ant.* XII.246; Jerome, *In Dan.* III.XI.14.
14 See V. Tcherikover, CPJ 1:11-5; A. Kasher, "First Jewish Military Units," 57-67.
15 *War* VII.432; *Ant.* XIII.64, 68; b *Menahot* 109b; p *Yoma* 6.3 (43d); Jerome, *In Dan.* III.XI.14.
16 For the textual variants in the city's name, see below, Chapter 6.4.
17 Cf. B. Duhm, *Das Buch Jesaia*, 120-1, with the previous note. M.D. McDonald, *The Prophetic Oracles*, 39-58, 137-46, 155-217, provides a useful analysis of Isaiah's Egyptian prophecies.

passage.[18] They may even have understood the subsequent verse (23)—
which speaks of Egypt's defeat by Assyria—as referring to the Sixth
Syrian War and Antiochus IV's two invasions of Egypt (170-168 BCE).[19]
But be that detail as it may, the Jewish refugees in Egypt, seeing the
Jerusalem temple contaminated—first by the service of illegitimate
priests and then by Antiochus' sacrilege—opted to build a new shrine,
thus fulfilling Isaiah's ancient prophecy.

From the authorities' point of view, there was every reason to
accept the Jews' wish to settle in Heliopolis. Egypt was still reeling from
the aftershocks of Antiochus' invasions, and Philometor knew that
Roman intervention—like the one of July 168—could not be counted on
if Antiochus' successors were to invade again. Settling a loyal foreign
unit in and around Heliopolis—a strategic point on the main road to
Memphis and Alexandria—was an important step toward defending
Egypt's heartland against further Syrian aggresion.[20]

A second threat to be reckoned with came from within the
Ptolemaic kingdom itself, for the 160s BCE had seen several dangerous
insurrections, not only in the rebellious south but in Lower Egypt as
well.[21] By letting Onias and his followers settle in the relatively
underdeveloped region of Heliopolis,[22] a short distance from Memphis,
Philometor was hoping that the Jews would keep an eye on the native
population, or, to use Josephus' words (speaking of an earlier period),

[18] For Isaiah's reputation as a trustworthy prophet of the *eschaton*, cf. Sir. 48:24-5.
[19] For a similar association in the book of Daniel, see H.L. Ginsberg, "The Oldest
Interpretation." For the equation between Syria and Assyria, cf. Th. Nöldke,
"ΑΣΣΥΡΙΟΣ ΣΥΡΙΟΣ ΣΥΡΟΣ."
[20] Heliopolis' strategic importance was recognized by Alexander (Arrian, *Anabasis*
III.1.3), Mithridates (see below), and Aurelian (?) (P.Leit. 9 (SB VIII, 10201)), as well
as the Arab, Turkish, and French invaders (see A.J. Butler, *The Arab Conquest*,
227-35; *Baedeker's Egypt 1929*, 129). Cf. Achilles Tatius, *LC* III.24.
[21] Diodorus XXXI.15a, 17a; Cl. Préaux, "Esquisse," 538-42; J.D. Ray, *The Archive of
Hor*, 129; B. Agnostou-Canas, "Rapports," 341-2, 346-7. The Oxyrhynchus fragment
of CPJ III, 520 (cf. G. Bohak, "CPJ III, 520," n. 4) seems to connect the Jews' arrival
in Heliopolis with the [στρα]τευμάτων στάσεις. I am grateful to Ludwig Koenen
for this information.
[22] Heliopolis, destroyed by the Persians (Strabo, *Geog.* XVII.1.27), was virtually
ignored by most earlier Ptolemies—see J. Yoyotte, "Prêtres et sanctuaires," 113-5
(for Manetho's supposed connection with Heliopolis see P.M. Fraser, *Ptolemaic
Alexandria*, 1:506, 2:729). In the Zenon archive and contemporary Greek papyri
Heliopolis figures as an area with some agricultural activity, but not much more,
and a similar picture emerges from the Demotic papyri. I am grateful to Janet
Johnson for allowing me access to the files of the Chicago Demotic Dictionary,
and to Karl-Theodor Zauzich for further assistance with Demotic place-names.

"he entrusted to (his Jewish subjects) the fortresses and the guarding thereof, so that they might fill the Egyptians with fear (τὰ φρούρια καὶ τὴν τούτων φυλακὴν παρέθετο, ἵνα τοῖς Αἰγυπτίοις ὦσιν φοβεροί)."[23] Philometor, then, was doing exactly what Antiochus IV had done in Jerusalem several years earlier, and what other Hellenistic rulers often did, namely, establishing a foreign military settlement in a strategic location to watch over the restive native population.[24]

There was, finally, a third reason for Onias' success. When Philometor returned to Egypt, in summer 163, he had reached a settlement with his brother, Ptolemy VIII Euergetes II, nicknamed Physcon, but there was no knowing how long the truce would last.[25] By granting his wishes, Philometor was securing Onias' loyalty to himself, and himself alone, in any future confrontation with his brother.

This, then, is the historical situation we are looking at: a young high priest's son, deprived of his hereditary rights in Jerusalem and eager to fulfill an ancient prophecy about a Jewish altar in Heliopolis, arrives in Egypt at a time of great external and internal upheaval. Ptolemy VI Philometor recruits this Judean refugee, along with all his followers, and grants them their wishes in exchange for allegiance and military service. Both sides seem to have been pleased with the results of their cooperation, and Josephus says that "Ptolemy Philometor and his wife Cleopatra entrusted their whole kingdom to Jews, and two Jews, Onias and Dositheus, were the commanders of their entire force (στρατηγοὶ πάσης τῆς δυνάμεως αὐτῶν)."[26] Josephus, who was unaware of it when writing his *War* and even when writing his *Antiquities*, clearly learned about this promotion from Apion's own work. Unfortunately, Apion's statement may have been a deliberate exaggeration, aimed at showing how Ptolemy VI caved in to the Jews,[27] and the identity of

---

23 *Ant.* XII.45, paraphrasing *Let. Arist.* 36, on Ptolemy I Soter. Cf. R. Marcus' note, LCL *Josephus*, 7:24-5.

24 For Antiochus IV's actions, see 1 Macc 1:33-6; Dan 11:39; Josephus, *Ant.* XII.252. For other examples, see, *Ant.* XII.147-53, with G.M. Cohen, *Seleucid Colonies*, 5-9 (Antiochus III); *Ag.Ap.* II.44 (Ptolemy I Soter), and *Ant.* XV.294 (Herod).

25 For this feud, see W. Otto, *Zur Geschichte der Zeit*, 92-5; E.S. Gruen, *The Hellenistic World*, 692-702, and L. Mooren, "Antiochos," 78-80.

26 *Ag.Ap.* II.49. The suggestion that this Onias is not the temple-builder (e.g., E.S. Gruen, "Origins and Objectives") seems highly unlikely in light of *Ant.* XIII.285-7, as well as the rarity of the name Onias in Ptolemaic Egpyt, with only three or four occurrences among the 17,000 persons listed in the *Prosopographia Ptolemaica*.

27 Cf. the claims of Apion's intellectual heirs that Trajan's συνέδριον was full of Jews (CPJ II, 157.42-50 = H. Musurillo, *Acta Alexandrinorum*, 34).

Onias' fellow-commander, Dositheus, also remains obscure.[28] What is clear, however, is that Onias was a protégé of the king and queen, and that this relationship made for a highly successful career in the Ptolemaic court.

2.1.3. The Land of Onias

When Onias came to Heliopolis, Josephus tells us, he received large tracts of land, to furnish material support for his temple and his men. This being a common Ptolemaic practice, there is little reason to doubt the veracity of Josephus' statement.[29] Unfortunately, our knowledge of ancient Heliopolis is very limited—the humidity of the soil prevents the preservation of papyri, and rapid urbanization precludes any extensive archeological excavations—and nothing is known about the size of the Oniad territories or the way they were administered.[30] Apparently, the area around Heliopolis became known as "the Land of Onias"—a name which was still in use long after Onias' death.[31] Moreover, the second century CE geographer Claudius Ptolemy implies that Heliopolis itself was renamed 'Ονίου, "Onias' (city),"[32] and his statement is corroborated by Eusebius and Jerome, who note that Onias' city was named after him.[33] The fact that Heliopolis' new name, Oniou (polis), was so similar

---

[28] It has been suggested that he was the son, or grandson, of the celebrated Dositheus son of Drimylos, or that he was the Dositheus mentioned in CPJ I, 24 as the commander of a cavalry unit in 174 BCE. For both suggestions, see E. van't Dack et al., The Judean-Syrian-Egyptian Conflict, 130-1.
[29] War VII.430. For Ptolemaic land-grants see, e.g., Cl. Préaux, L'Économie royale, 463-80; for temple lands, see W. Otto, Priester und Tempel, 1:262-82.
[30] The available literary and papyrological evidence for Greco-Roman Heliopolis is conveniently listed in Calderini's Dizionario, 2:203-5; Suppl. 1:124. See also J. Yoyotte, "Prêtres et sanctuaires," 113-5; H. Ricke, "Hohe Sand;" id., "Inventartafel;" Porter-Moss, Topographical Bibliography, 4:59-65; A.-A. Saleh, Excavations at Heliopolis. For the most recent excavations, see the brief notices in the BIA and the periodic surveys by J. Leclant and G. Clerc in Orientalia. I am grateful to Carol Redmount and Jeffrey Spencer for their comments on Heliopolitan archeology.
[31] Josephus, War I.190; Ant. XIII.287; XIV.131; JIGRE 38 (CIJ 1530, purchased in Cairo): Φαμισθὰ δ' 'Ονίου γᾶ τροφὸς ἀμετέρα.
[32] Cl. Ptol., Geog. IV.5.53: Ἡλιοπολίτης νομός καὶ μητρόπολις Ἡλίου ἢ 'Ονίου. Ptolemy also mentions a second Heliopolis, to the south-east of 'Ονίου, in the eastern desert—see the map in J. Ball, Egypt, 117.
[33] Eusebius, Chronica (ed. Schoene), 2:126: 'Ονείας... ἐλθὼν εἰς Αἴγυπτον κτίζει πόλιν τὴν ἐπικληθεῖσαν 'Ονείου. Jerome's translation (ibid., 127; ed. Helm, 141): "Onias... in Heliopolitano pago civitatem nominis sui condit;" Jerome, In Dan. III.XI.14:

to its ancient Egyptian name, *iwnw* (Hebrew אֹון, LXX 'Ων, Coptic ωΝ), is, of course, a mere coincidence, but Onias' followers might have seen in this a sign of divine providence—Onias' arrival being somehow "foretold" in the city's Egyptian name.[34]

Onias and his followers settled not in one, but several locations, in and around Heliopolis (cf. the map at the end of this study).[35] The Jewish epitaphs from Tell-el-Yahoudieh certainly belong to an Oniad settlement, as do the remarkably similar epitaphs found at Demerdash, some four km south of Heliopolis.[36] To these two a third settlement might be added, namely, "the Jews' Camp" ('Ιουδαίων στρατόπεδον), on the western side of the Nile, near the crossing point below the Delta.[37] A second site known as Tell-el-Yahoud, twenty-one km north-east of the first, may have been another Oniad settlement.[38] Finally, in a papyrus dated 59 CE we hear of three Jews who lived in the Syrians' Village not far from Babylon. This last location probably should be identified with the village Siryaqus, mentioned in Coptic and Arabic sources and still noted on maps of modern Egypt.[39] In line with this geographic diffusion, we may note one Jewish epitaph that describes the deceased, Abramos, as "having been the *politarch* in two different places (δισσῶν τόπων

"urbs, quae vocabatur Oniae." Cf. the fragmentary Tell-el-Yahoudieh inscription which reads]'Ονίου πατήρ [, possibly referring to one of the city's leaders (JIGRE 44 (CIJ 1455)).

[34] H. Kees' ("'Ονίου," 479) and A. Barucq's ("Léontopolis," 365) suggestion that 'Ονίου is merely the Greek form of the Egyptian *iwnw* is linguistically improbable and historically unwarranted ('Ονίου being the genetive of Onias' name).

[35] Josephus (*War* I.175; cf. *Ant*. XIV.99; *Ag.Ap*. II.64) notes that Pelusium too was occupied by Jews, without, however, supplying any further details.

[36] For Tell-el-Yahoudieh, see below, nn. 46-7. One should note, however, that the real origins of many of the inscriptions attributed to Tell-el-Yahoudieh remain unknown—e.g., JIGRE 30, 31, 32, 33 etc. (cf. G. Bohak, "Good Jews, Bad Jews"). For Demerdash, see C.C. Edgar, "A Group of Inscriptions," 32-8; JIGRE, xvi-xix.

[37] *War* I.190; *Ant*. XIV.133. For its location, cf. P.J. Sijpesteijn, "Mithridates' March," 122-7, and A. Kasher, *The Jews*, 121-2 with Schürer (rev.), *History*, 3:48-9.

[38] For this second Tell-el-Yahoud, ten km south of Bilbeis, see E. Naville, *Mound of the Jew*, 23. As noted by J. Lesquier, *L'armée romaine*, 392, n. 2, it is probably this second Tell-el-Yahoudieh which should be equated with the *Vicus Iudaeorum* of the *Itinerarium Antonini* 169 (ed. Miller, lix). The *castra Iudaeorum* mentioned in the *Notitia Dignitatum* XXVIII.42 (ed. Seeck, 60) must be identical with one of the Tell-el-Yahoud(ieh)s—see Schürer (rev.), *History*, 3:48.

[39] CPJ II, 417: 'Ιουδαῖοι... τῶν [ἀ]πὸ Σύρων κώμης. Cf. G. Vaggi, "Siria e Siri," 32, and A. Calderini, *Dizionario*, 4:323. For Siryaqus, see S. Timm, *Christlische-koptische Ägypten*, 2369-70.

πολιταρχῶν)"—presumably, he held a magistracy in two neighboring Oniad settlements.[40] It is, finally, not impossible that Onias wished to build exactly five "cities" in Egypt, in line with Isa 19:18, but the establishment of several small settlements clustered in one region is well known from other Hellenistic military colonies, and is hardly unusual.[41]

Noting the extensive Oniad presence in the Heliopolite region, we would not be surprised to read Strabo's brief statement, quoted by Josephus, that "In Egypt there is a Jewish settlement which is assigned to them alone (ἐν γοῦν Αἰγύπτῳ κατοικία τῶν Ἰουδαίων ἐστὶν ἀποδεδειγμένη χωρὶς)." Apparently, Strabo was referring to the Land of Onias—of which he had spoken elsewhere in his historical work—for there was no other area in Egypt set aside for a Jewish settlement.[42] Heliopolis, it seems, was a safe haven for the many refugees from Judea.

2.1.4. The Temple: Location and Appearance

While the Jewish presence in several locations within the Heliopolite region is relatively well documented, the exact location of their temple remains unknown. This is a tricky question, especially because of earlier scholars' claim to have identified the remains of Onias' temple in Tell-el-Yahoudieh. Assuming that Onias had built his temple in "Leontopolis of the Heliopolite nome," and that Tell-el-Yahoudieh is where the temple was located, they equated Tell-el-Yahoudieh with "Leontopolis," and pronounced the problem solved.[43] Both assumptions, however, are at best doubtful. First, it must be stressed that a Heliopolitan "Leontopolis" is only mentioned in Onias' and Philometor's purported correspondence (*Ant.* XIII.65-71). Yet these letters are obvious forgeries, aimed at undermining the legitimacy of Onias' temple by portraying it as inherently impure, and probably written no earlier than the Roman

---

[40] Cf. JIGRE 39, with L. Robert, "Epigramme," 21-4, and P.W. van der Horst, "Jewish Poetical Tomb Inscriptions," 134-5.
[41] Cf. *Ant.* XII.149; XVII.26; G.M. Cohen, "The Hellenistic Military Colony," 87-8.
[42] *Ant.* XIV.117. For Strabo's reports on Oniad matters, cf. *Ant.* XIII.286-7.
[43] Unfortunately, many maps of ancient Egypt take this equation for granted and identify Tell-el-Yahoudieh as "Leontopolis"—e.g., JIGRE, pl. 1; J. Mélèze Modrzejewski, *Les juifs d'Egypte*, 205. Some maps identify the site both as "Tell-el-Yahoudieh" and as "Leontopolis," a practice which is somewhat less misleading—e.g., Baines-Malek, *Atlas*, 166-7; A. Kasher, *The Jews*, 109; E. van't Dack *et al.*, *The Judean-Syrian-Egyptian Conflict*, 163.

period.[44] Of course, it is not impossible that a forgery would contain a correct reference to the temple's location, but this certainly cannot be taken for granted. Josephus himself, we may add, never refers to "Leontopolis" as the location of Onias' temple, and prefers the more ambiguous "in the Heliopolite nome"—even after quoting Onias' and Philometor's letters! In this, he is followed by all the Christian writers who mention Onias' temple. They too always refer to Heliopolis and ignore the Heliopolitan "Leontopolis"—a site which, in fact, is never mentioned by any other source.[45]

In addition to this first difficulty regarding "Leontopolis," it is also doubtful whether Onias' temple was situated in Tell-el-Yahoudieh at all. Unfortunately, the structure identified by Flinders Petrie as Onias' temple has all but disintegrated, yet his own description thereof makes the identification highly improbable.[46] With all due respect to this founding father of Egyptian archeology, we must agree with the most recent study of the Jews of ancient Egypt that "Contrairement à ce que croyait l'archéologue britannique Flinders Petrie, on n'en (i.e., Onias' temple) a jamais retrouvé le moindre vestige."[47] Moreover, it must be stressed—and has been stressed by scholars long before Petrie's time—that according to the available evidence Onias' temple should not have been located at Tell-el-Yahoudieh in the first place.[48] Josephus (*War*

---

[44] See S. Krauss, "Leontopolis," 7-8; B. Motzo, *Saggi di storia*, 183; V. Tcherikover, *Hellenistic Civilization*, 499 nn. 29-30; M. Delcor, "le temple d'Onias," 194-5; E.S. Gruen, "Origins and Objectives." For the date, L. Robert, *Études épigraphiques*, 235. Note also the striking verbal similarity between *Ant.* XIII.68 and IX.242.

[45] *War* I.33; VII.426; *Ant.* XII.388; XIII.285; XX.236; A. Barucq, "Léontopolis," 366-7. Unfortunately, some scholars still confuse the well known Leontopolis (Tell-Muqdam) with Josephus' "Leontopolis" (e.g., B.-Z. Wacholder, *Eupolemus*, 164; Merkelbach-Totti, *Abrasax*, 1:78).

[46] For the excavations at Tell-el-Yahoudieh, see E. Brugsch-Bey, "On;" E. Naville, *Mound of the Jew*; F.L. Griffith, *Antiquities*; W.M. Flinders Petrie, *Hyksos*; *id.*, *Egypt and Israel*, 97-180; Du Mesnil du Buisson, "Compte rendu sommaire;" *id.*, "Le temple d'Onias;" Porter-Moss, *Topographic Bibliography*, 4:56-9; Sh. Adam, "Recent Discoveries," 305, 308-14; G.R.H. Wright, "Tell el-Yahoudiah," 1-7. Gardiner's identification (*Ancient Egyptian Onomastica*, 146-9; cf. W. Helck, "Natho," 354-5) of Tell-el-Yahoudieh with the Ναθῶ of Herodotus II.165 and PSI V, 543 is far from certain—cf. also A.B. Lloyd, *Herodotus Book II*, 3:189. For "Natho" in Coptic sources, see S. Timm, *Christliche-koptische Ägypten*, 1490-3.

[47] J. Mélèze Modrzejewski, *Les juifs d'Egypte*, 106. Cf. Du Mesnil du Buisson, "Le temple d'Onias," 59-64; M. Delcor, "Le temple d'Onias," 204-5 (a postscript by R. de Vaux); R. Hayward, "The Jewish Temple," 431; JIGRE, xvii; A. Zivie, "Tell el Yahoudieh," 11.

[48] See, e.g., Fourmont, *Description historique*, 199.

VII.426) states that Onias' temple was situated 180 *stadia*, or 22.5
Roman miles, away from Memphis, a detail probably derived from the
reports of the Roman units who destroyed the temple (see below), and
who had precise knowledge of its location. Since other Roman sources
state that the distance between Memphis and Heliopolis itself was 24
miles,[49] it seems clear that Onias' temple was located inside, or very
close to, ancient Heliopolis. While Tell-el-Yahoudieh certainly was an
Oniad settlement, Onias' temple probably was located elsewhere.
Unfortunately, its exact location is unknown, and given the current state
of ancient Heliopolis and its environs the chances that the temple's
remains will ever be found seem hopelessly dim.[50] In this, however,
Onias' temple is not alone, for neither the Jewish temple at Elephantine
nor the Samaritan temple on Mount Gerizim have securely been
identified, in spite of much archeological effort.

But what did this temple look like? Josephus, our main source,
gives us conflicting accounts on this score. At the beginning of the *War*
(I.33), he says that Onias' temple was modeled after the one in
Jerusalem.[51] In *War* VII.427, however, he claims that Onias' temple was
"not like the one in Jerusalem, but resembled a tower of large stones,
sixty cubits high (πύργῳ παραπλήσιον λίθων μεγάλων εἰς ἑξήκοντα πή-
χεις ἀνεστηκότα)." To understand the roots of this contradiction we must
recall that the Jerusalem temple itself had undergone a massive
reconstruction, initiated by Herod, which turned it into a much larger
edifice than it had previously been. Originally, it was 60 cubits high and
60 cubits wide (Ezra 6:3), and resembled a tower—this, at least, is the
image used in some contemporary literature.[52] In the process of the
Herodian reconstruction, however, its height was raised from 60 to 100
cubits, and two "shoulders" were added to it, one on each side, so that
the building looked, in the Mishna's poetic expression, "like a lion," for
it was "narrow on the rear and wide on the front" (m *Middot* 4:6-7; cf.

---

[49] *Itinerarium Antonini*, 163 (ed. Miller, lix), supported by the fourth-century
pilgrim Egeria (J. Wilkinson, *Egeria's Travels*, 204).
[50] For Heliopolis' sad fate, see the brief remarks of A. Nibbi, "The Eastern Delta,"
and A.-P. Zivie, "Préservation."
[51] Cf. Eusebius, *Chronica* (ed. Schoene), 2:126: Ὀνείας... ἱερὸν οἰκοδομεῖ ὅμοιον τοῦ
ναοῦ τοῦ ἐν Ἱεροσολύμοις, and Jerome, *In Dan*. III.XI.14: "Onias sacerdos...
templum exstruxit in Aegypto simile templi Iudaeorum...".
[52] See *1 Enoch* 89:50, 73 and the *variae lectiones* in LXX Sir 49:12. Cf. also *Sib. Or.*
V.422-5. R. Hayward, "The Jewish Temple," 432-4, and M. Delcor, "Sanctuaires
juifs," 1320-1, adduce further references to later sources.

War V.207). Onias' temple, a tower 60 cubits high, was built as a replica of the Jerusalem temple, and was described as such by pre-Herodian witnesses.[53] Later visitors, however, including the Roman forces who eventually destroyed Onias' temple, correctly noted that it differed in shape and size from the one in Jerusalem. Josephus, using pre-Herodian sources at the beginning of the *War* and contemporary accounts in *War* VII.420-36, was inattentive to their mutual inconsistencies, and so he first said that Onias' temple looked like the Jerusalem temple, and then said that it did not. When writing the *Antiquities*, some twenty years later, he said that Onias' temple was similar to the one in Jerusalem (*Ant*. XII.388; XIII.63, 67, 285; XX.236), but added that it was "smaller and poorer" (*Ant*. XIII.72)—it was, he knew, only 60 cubits high, 40 cubits less than the one in Jerusalem.

The claim that Onias modeled his temple after the one in Jerusalem finds support from one additional source. In the Greek version of Isaiah 19:18, the verse which motivated Onias' settlement in Heliopolis, we find an important change—the city's name is translated as πόλις ασεδεκ.[54] As has often been noted, this minor change effectively equates Onias' city with "the City of Righteousness" (עיר הצדק) of Isaiah 1:26.[55] If Onias and his supporters indeed viewed their new city, and not Jerusalem, as the true "City of Righteousness" promised by Isaiah, they had a strong incentive to model it after the city they left behind.

2.2. The Subsequent History of Onias' Temple

Having discussed the establishment of Onias' temple at some length, we must now try to reconstruct its subsequent history. Unfortunately, the data at our disposal are extremely limited. Josephus, our main source, mentions only three incidents connected with the Land of Onias and its inhabitants, and these brief accounts must serve as the basis for any reconstruction of Oniad history.

---

[53] As was the Samaritan temple on Mt. Gerizim—*War* I.63; *Ant*. XI.310; XIII.256.
[54] Attested in most LXX mss. A variant reading—πόλις ασεδ ήλίου—is probably secondary, conflating ασεδεκ with ῾Ηλίου (πόλις).
[55] See M. Delcor, "Le temple d'Onias," 201, and below, Chapter 6.4.

2.2.1. Onias and Physcon (145 BCE)

The first of these events occurred in 145 BCE, immediately after Philometor's death. Josephus does not mention this event in the *War*, nor in the *Antiquities*, but in his subsequent work, *Against Apion*, he discusses this episode, which Apion had used as grist for his anti-Jewish mill. Josephus relates that following Philometor's death, when the Alexandrians were bent on fighting the widowed queen, Cleopatra II, it was Onias and Dositheus who brokered a truce and saved the city from civil war (*Ag. Ap.* II.50). Moreover, when the deceased king's brother, Physcon, left Cyrene—where he had ruled since his ouster from Egypt in 163 BCE—and marched on Alexandria, wishing to regain the crown, Onias took Cleopatra's side and mobilized his forces. Preparing for a confrontation, Physcon arrested the Jews of Alexandria and threatened to have them trampled upon by his elephants. His plans were thwarted, however, by the elephants' refusal to cooperate, by his concubine's appeal to forego such impiety, and by a terrible apparition which he saw—this, at least, is Josephus' account (*ibid.*, 50-6). Be this as it may, Josephus' claim that the Jews of Alexandria still maintain an annual celebration commemorating their miraculous deliverance finds support in 3 Maccabees' account of the same events (esp. 3 Macc 6:36), in spite of the latter work's attempt to date these events many years earlier and thus rid them of any Oniad connection. From other sources, moreover, we know that the conflict between Physcon and Cleopatra ended in a typical compromise—a marriage and joint rule of Egypt—which presumably eased the tensions between Physcon and his Jewish subjects and gave rise to the story of their miraculous deliverance.[56]

The events of 145 BCE, obscure as they are, present us with some very telling lessons. First, we learn that Philometor had been right in trusting Onias and his followers—in Cleopatra's time of trouble, Onias showed his loyalty, taking great risks in supporting his former patron's widow. Second, we learn that Onias had quite a formidable force at his disposal, and was deeply involved in the power-struggles of the Ptolemaic court. Third, we learn that, at least from Physcon's point of view, the Jewish community of Alexandria was intimately connected

---

[56] See Otto-Bengtson, *Zur Geschichte*, 24-9; V. Tcherikover, CPJ 1:21-3; Schürer (rev.), *History*, 3:539. Cf. A. Kasher, *The Jews*, 211-32, who prefers 3 Maccabees' account, and M. Chauveau, "Un été 145," 161-3, who adopts an entirely different chronology.

with Onias and his forces—he could use Alexandrian Jews as "human shields," as it were, against Onias' men.

After these events, the Oniad settlements and their inhabitants disappear from our sight for quite a while. It is possible that an Oniad force was involved once again when the war between Physcon and his sister-wife erupted anew, in 132/1 BCE—but given the paucity of the evidence, this must remain no more than a plausible conjecture.[57] There is, in fact, no direct evidence to shed light on the relations between Physcon, whose reign lasted to 116 BCE, and Onias (or his descendants), in the period following this brief confrontation.

2.2.2. Ananias and Jerusalem (103 BCE)

By 103 BCE, more than a decade after Physcon's death, the scene has utterly changed.[58] Cleopatra III (Physcon's second wife) was the sole ruler, Onias IV was dead, and his two sons, Chelkias and Ananias, were prominent generals in Cleopatra's army. Both served—until Chelkias' death in mid-campaign—as joint commanders of her Syrian expedition, aimed against her own son, Ptolemy Lathyrus (*Ant.* XIII.285, 348-51). Following her successful siege of Ptolemais (Acco), Cleopatra was approached by Alexander Janneus, whose request for her allegiance was accompanied by costly gifts. Some of her advisors suggested that she should accept Alexander's gifts, and then invade his country—but Ananias objected, and convinced the queen to abandon any such plan. Following his advice, she made an alliance with Alexander, thus giving him the freedom to embark on a new set of conquests (*ibid.*, 353-64).

Josephus' description of these events provides us with much useful evidence. First, we learn that Onias' high rank was passed on to his sons—they held in Cleopatra III's court a position similar to what he and Dositheos had held in Philometor's court half a century earlier.[59] Second, we learn that these two wielded a great deal of influence with the queen, as even Strabo readily admits (*Ant.* XIII.287). Third, we learn that they were deeply involved in the queen's adventure—so involved,

---

[57] See Otto-Bengtson, *Zur Geschichte*, 56-70, and M. Stern, "The Relations," 94-5.
[58] For what follows, see E. van't Dack *et al.*, *The Judean-Syrian-Egyptian Conflict*.
[59] Note also the mention of a Χελκίου γῆ in the Busirite nome in 13 BCE (CPJ II, 145), which Chelkias may have received in return for his services—but this may have been another Chelkias (see below).

in fact, that Chelkias lost his life fighting on her behalf, so far away from home. Fourth, and this is the most important point, we learn that Ananias declined an offer to attack Jerusalem.

The significance of this event cannot be overstated, for while Alexander's forces were far from negligible, there is little doubt that a concentrated effort on Cleopatra's part to recapture the Ptolemies' long-lost Palestinian possessions would have posed a severe threat to this newly-crowned king, who had just been defeated by Lathyrus in battle (*Ant.* XIII.326-44). What Ananias was being offered, then, was an opportunity to take Jerusalem, reclaim the high priestly post which his father was denied, and return things to the way they were throughout the third century BCE, with Jerusalem ruled by an Oniad high priest and paying taxes to a Ptolemaic master.

Such prospects must have seemed quite tempting to Ananias—but he declined, and convinced the queen to abandon this bold plan. What exactly stood behind his refusal to attack, and the *de facto* recognition of the Hasmonean control of Jerusalem and its temple, we may never know. It is possible that Josephus' explanation—that Ananias assumed that the Jews of Egypt would not support such an unprovoked attack on Jerusalem—is indeed correct.[60] It is also possible that Ananias knew that the changing political climate within Judea—the Sadducees, his natural allies, having made peace with John Hyrcanus, Alexander's father—would make it virtually impossible for him to find any supporters there.[61] It is even possible that his calculations focused on the larger scene, assuming that the Romans would never let Cleopatra annex Judea, and that any such adventure was doomed to fail.[62]

Regardless of its motives, Ananias' reluctance to attack signals his recognition that the Jerusalem temple, the center of an independent, vibrant, and expanding kingdom, was now the unrivaled focal-point of all Jewish allegiance. If we recall that in the 140s BCE the Hasmoneans were only beginning to consolidate their power, that only in 128 did they manage to destroy the rival center on Mount Gerizim, and that in 124 they still had to cajole the Jews of Egypt to celebrate the re-dedication of the Jerusalem temple (2 Macc 1:1-9), then we realize that a great change

---

[60] See M. Stern, "The Relations," 101, who adds Ananias' own sense of "Jewish solidarity."

[61] See *Ant.* XIII.288-98, with Schürer (rev.), *History*, 1:210-4, and L.I. Levine, "The Political Struggle," 78-9.

[62] M. Stern, "The Relations," 102.

had taken place in 103 BCE, with Ananias' fateful decision. This was, in fact, the Oniads' last chance to dislodge the Hasmoneans and regain their former position. Once this opportunity came and went, the Oniads, and their Heliopolitan temple, were consigned to oblivion.

Onias' temple was not deserted, of course, and it is quite probable that Chelkias' and Ananias' descendants passed its high priesthood smoothly from one generation to the next. An extremely mutilated inscription, bought in Cairo almost a century ago, records how "those in the sacred precinct (...πλή]θους τῶν ἐν τῷ τεμέ[νει...)"—presumably, Onias' temple—honored their leader with a golden crown. Chelkias' name is mentioned (...] Χελκίου στ[ρατηγοῦ...), but the fragmentary nature of the inscription precludes any certainty as to whether the honoree was Chelkias himself or a later, homonymous descendant.[63]

In addition to this inscription, two other documents might be connected with Onias' descendants. The first is a petition addressed "to Chelkias the strategos (Χελκίαι στρατηγῶι)" that can be dated, on the basis of paleography, to no earlier than the mid-first century BCE.[64] Its provenance is unknown—Herakleopolis has been suggested—and its value is rather limited. It is likely that this Chelkias too was a Jew—the name is unattested among non-Jews—and he may even have been a descendant, perhaps even a grandson, of Onias IV's son, becoming a strategos (of the Heliopolite nome?) in line with family tradition. Without further evidence, however, these must remain no more than plausible hypotheses.

A second source which might be relevant here is a long land register, dated ca. 47 CE, which mentions "Iason, a former strategos," perhaps of the Heliopolite nome (the reading is uncertain).[65] If "Heliopolis" indeed is the correct reading, this Iason may have been a Jew (the name was popular among Jews, though never limited to Jews alone), and perhaps even a descendant of Onias himself (Iason, of course, was Onias IV's uncle, and the name may have run in the family). This too, however, is no more than an intriguing possibility.

---

63 JIGRE 129 (CIJ 1450). For the τέμενος of Onias' temple, see *War* VII.429, 434 and Th. Reinach, "Un préfet juif," 52. See also U. Rappaport, "Les Iduméens en Égypte," 80-2.
64 P.Med. inv. 69.59 (SB XIV, 11269). See Hagedorn-Sijpesteijn, "Die Stadtviertel," 103-4. I am grateful to Dieter Hagedorn for discussing this document with me.
65 P.Lond. III, 604B.240 (with the editors' note *ad loc.*); cf. Bastianini-Whitehorne, *Strategi*, 62.

2.2.3. Helping Julius Caesar (48/7 BCE)

Following Ananias' fateful decision of 103 BCE, the Oniad settlements disappear from our sight for a period of some sixty years. It is possible, but far from certain, that the Oniad Jews were involved in the "Jewish support (ʾΙουδαϊκὰς ἐπικουρίας)" for Ptolemy Alexander I (107-88 BCE) against his brother Ptolemy Lathyrus, mentioned by Porphyry.[66] It is also possible that the Jewish notables who fled Jerusalem in 65 BCE—when Hyrcanus II was besieging his brother Aristoboulus II in the temple— and celebrated the Passover holiday in Egypt, were doing so in Onias' temple.[67] Once again, however, the evidence is too vague to allow any certain reconstruction of these obscure events.

The next episode in Oniad history of which we are well informed comes in 48/7 BCE, during Caesar's Alexandrian war.[68] Besieged within the city, Caesar was waiting for the auxiliary forces recruited by Mithridates, who was marching from Pergamon to Egypt, accompanied by Antipater, Herod's father. The two arrived in Pelusium, conquered it, and entered Egypt, but in the Land of Onias their advance was blocked by the local Jewish forces. These were mollified only after Antipater's intervention "on the ground of their common nationality (κατὰ τὸ ὁμόφυλον)," and following his assurance that their march was supported by Hyrcanus II, the high priest in Jerusalem.[69] The Oniad settlers, it seems, still retained some strength as late as 47 BCE, and Heliopolis' strategic location made their consent to Mithridates' march essential.[70] Yet Josephus—who is clearly using Nicolaus of Damascus' account of these events—depicts the Oniad Jews as entirely subordinate to their brethren in Jerusalem. On the eve of the Roman conquest, these Jews formed a small military force that could prevent a foreign militia from passing through Heliopolis, but had no real impact on Ptolemaic history, and no independent position vis-à-vis Jerusalem. Little wonder, then, that some seven years later Cleopatra VII would offer the command of

---

[66] *Apud* Eusebius, *Chronica* (ed. Schoene), 1:166; cf. M. Stern, *Greek and Latin Authors*, 2:444-6, and *id.*, "The Relations," 103-4.
[67] See *Ant.* XIV.21, with Schürer (rev.), *History*, 1:235-6, and H. Tchernowitz, "The Pairs," 236.
[68] For what follows, see esp. P.J. Sijpesteijn, "Mithridates' March," 122-7.
[69] *Ant.* XIV.131-2; *War* I.190. Cf. also *Ag.Ap.* II.61.
[70] Note, however, that while Josephus emphasizes the Jews' role in these events (cf. *Ant.* XIV.137-9, 193), neither the *Bellum Alexandrinum* (see esp. XXVI.3) nor Dio Cassius (XLII.41-3) ever mention it.

an expedition which she was preparing not to one of Onias' descendants, but to Herod, a Jewish refugee from Palestine (*War* I.279).

Caesar's campaign over, we now hear nothing concerning the Land of Onias for the next one hundred twenty years. To be sure, Jews still lived in the Heliopolite nome, and many of the epitaphs from Tell-el-Yahoudieh and Demerdash probably date from this period.[71] One such inscription, purchased in the vicinity of Tell-el-Yahoudieh and securely dated to 27 BCE, is the tombstone of "Marin, the priestess (Μάριν ἱερισ⟨σ⟩α)"—a title which, to judge from its appearance in Jewish inscriptions from Rome, Beth She'arim, and Jerusalem, denoted priestly heritage rather than active priestly service.[72] But the male members of Marin's family probably did serve in Onias' temple, even in this period of rapid change and irreversible decline.

With the Roman conquest of Egypt, in 30 BCE, the Oniad Jews lost whatever influence they still had by virtue of their military strength and strategic location. The Romans had little use for the foreign soldier-settlers imported by the Ptolemies, and no fear of invasions from the north, as both Syria and Palestine were firmly in their hands. Neglecting the Heliopolite nome, they garrisoned at Babylon (Old Cairo) instead—from which they could control the Nile valley, the all-important corn transport, and the Egyptian center in Memphis. Heliopolis itself now was no more than a quarry from which to ship Pharaonic obelisks to Alexandria or Rome.[73] Strabo, accompanying the prefect Aelius Gallus on his tour of Egypt (25 BCE), describes Heliopolis as "entirely deserted (πανέρημος)," with only a few priests and some tourist-guides present (*Geog.* XVII.1.27-9). The Land of Onias and its temple—which Strabo had mentioned in his historical writings—apparently were not deemed worthy of Gallus' inspection or Strabo's description. In Egypt, a temple sixty cubits high was nothing to be impressed by, and a Jewish temple—in a country which hosted Greek, Syrian, Phoenician, Idumean, and other foreign temples—was no cause for a detour, not even a short one.

---

71 See J. Mélèze Modrzejewski, *Les juifs d'Egypte*, 108-11, and D. Noy, "The Jewish Communities."

72 JIGRE 84 (CIJ 1514). See CIJ 315 (Rome); CIJ 1007 (Beth She'arim), and Avni *et al.*, "Three new Burial Caves," 105 (Jerusalem). Cf. B.J. Brooten, *Women Leaders*, 78-95, esp. 88-90.

73 For Babylon, see Strabo, *Geog.* XVII.1.30; J. Lesquier, *L'armée romaine*, 394-5. For the obelisks, Strabo, *Geog.* XVII.1.27; Ammianus Marcellinus, XVII.4.12; E.P. Uphill, "Pithom and Raamses," 35; L. Kákosy, "Heliopolis," 1112.

In 20 BCE, several years after Strabo's visit, Egypt's temples were dealt a heavy blow. To curtail their power, Augustus ordered the confiscation of all temple land throughout Egypt, making them entirely dependent on leases or subventions from the royal treasury. This bold reform had a palpable impact on the Egyptian temples, which went through a period of rapid decline, and may have had a similar impact on Onias' temple.[74] Coupled with the general decline in the fortunes of Egypt's Jews under Roman rule,[75] the effect of Roman legislation on Onias' temple must have been devastating. Thus, it comes as no surprise that Philo, our major source for Egyptian Jewish history and culture of the first century CE, does not even mention that temple. In fact, were it not for the destruction of Onias' temple in the aftermath of the Great Jewish Revolt, we might have known something about the Jews of the Heliopolite nome,[76] but not about their temple.

2.3. The Destruction of Onias' Temple (74 CE)

One interesting aspect of Josephus' War is that it opens and ends with Onias' temple. At the very beginning of his historical narrative (War I.31-3), Josephus mentions Onias' escape to Egypt and the construction of his temple there, adding that "We shall return to these matters in due course." This promise is fulfilled only at the very end of his work, when he describes how Onias' temple was destroyed by the Romans. After depicting the conquest of Jerusalem and the destruction of its temple, Josephus describes the war's final episodes—the siege and conquest of Masada (VII.252-406), the escape of some of the Zealots to Egypt, the trouble which they caused there, and the cruel punishments which the Romans inflicted upon them (VII.407-19). It is at this point that he finally returns to Onias' temple, relating how Vespasian, "suspicious of the Jews' constant rebelliousness, and fearing lest they gather together again all in one place (μὴ πάλιν εἰς ἓν ἀθρόοι συλλεγῶσι) drawing others with them," ordered Lupus, the *praefectus Aegypti* from 71 to 73 or 74

---

[74] See A.C. Johnson, *Roman Egypt*, 122-4, 639-49; J.E.G. Whitehorne, "New Light," 219-21; D.J. Thompson, *Memphis*, 271-6.

[75] See V.A. Tcherikover, "The Decline of the Jewish Diaspora in Egypt," and J. Mélèze Modrzejewski, *Les juifs d'Egypte*, 131-5.

[76] Such as the three Jews from the Syrians' Village, who appear in a loan-contract of 59 CE (CPJ II, 417). The name Chelkias, which ran in the borrowers' family, could support the suggestion that they were descendants of the Oniad settlers.

CE,[77] to destroy Onias' temple (*War* VII.421). Lupus merely shut down the temple and despoiled some of its appurtenances, but Paulinus, his successor, completely stripped the temple of all its treasures, "prohibited would-be worshipers from as much as entering the temple precincts (οὔτε προσιέναι τῷ τεμένει τοὺς θρησκεύειν βουλομένους ἀφῆκεν)," and barred all access to the structure. This, at least, is Josephus' account (*ibid.*, 433-5), and while his familiarity with accurate Roman reports of this recent event is beyond doubt, his claim that the temple merely was shut down merits little faith.[78] First, Josephus himself admits that Paulinus "made sure that not even a trace of the divine worship was left in that place (ὡς μηδ' ἴχνος ἔτι τῆς εἰς τὸν θεὸν θεραπείας ἐν τῷ τόπῳ καταλιπεῖν)" (*ibid.*, 435). Second, other sources are more explicit. The Targum (Ps.-Jonathan) to Isa 19:18 "updates" that prophecy by referring to the Jewish altar in "the city of Heliopolis, which will be destroyed (קרתא דבית שמש דעתידא למחרב)."[79] Jerome states that Onias' city "was razed to the ground," and that its temple was destroyed.[80] Finally, a difficult passage in the *Fifth Sibylline Oracle* (493-511) speaks of a Jewish temple which would one day be built in Egypt, and how it would later be destroyed—a description which seems to have been influenced by the fate of Onias' temple.[81]

Why the Romans destroyed this temple is far from clear. As early as 71/2 CE they were collecting the "Jewish tax" in Egypt—the Jews' voluntary half-shekel temple-tax, which, following the destruction of the Jerusalem temple, was collected by the Romans and sent to Rome.[82] Apparently, they took it for granted that the Egyptian Jews formerly paid their temple-tax to the Jerusalem temple, and ignored Onias' temple—otherwise, they would not have forced the Jews to pay the

---

[77] For Ti. Iulius Lupus and (Valerius) Paulinus, see P. Bureth, "Le préfet d'Egypte," 479-80; G. Bastianini, "Lista," 275; *id.*, "Lista... correzioni," 78; *id.*, "Il prefetto," 506; P.J. Sijpesteijn, "Flavius Josephus," 117-25, and D.B. Campbell, "Dating," 156-8.

[78] For Josephus' attempts to absolve his patrons, Vespasian and Titus, from the sacrilege of temple-destruction, cf. G. Alon, "The Burning of the Temple."

[79] B.D. Chilton, *The Isaiah Targum*, 39. R.P. Gordon's suggestion ("Terra Sancta," 123-4) that the Aramaic translator inserted anti-Oniad propaganda into his verse is less likely, given the late date of the Isaiah Targum.

[80] Jerome, *In Dan.* III.XI.14: "ipsa autem urbs... ad solum usque deleta est... et templum et urbs postea detruentur."

[81] See, e.g., J.J. Collins, "The Sibylline Oracles," 405; but note J. Geffcken, *Komposition*, 26, who denies this connection. For the text, see also PSI III, 389.

[82] For the "Jewish tax" receipts, see CPJ 2:112-36, and L.S. Wallace, *Taxation*, 170-6.

"Jewish tax" when Onias' temple was still standing. On the other hand, Josephus' claim that Vespasian feared lest the Zealots who escaped from Judea, together with their Egyptian brethren, would all unite in Onias' temple, implies that at least some Jews now saw that temple as the center of their religious and political aspirations. The Romans, sensing a potential for trouble, opted for what we would now call a "preemptive surgical strike," and the temple's two hundred and forty year history came to an ignoble end.[83]

The temple lay in ruins, but the Jewish settlements of the Heliopolite nome went on with their daily lives for at least another forty years. They were finally decimated, along with the other Jews of Egypt, in the great massacre which followed the Jewish revolt of 115-117 CE, the final chapter in the history of Egypt's Hellenistic Jews.[84] Soon after that event—probably in Hadrian's reign—we hear of a re-settlement of this ancient town by Egyptians and Greeks.[85]

Onias' temple has left no physical traces,[86] but the memory of its existence, dim as it was, did not completely vanish. The rabbis, who erroneously assumed the temple to have been built by Onias III and to have been located in Alexandria, debated at some length whether it was permissible to fulfill a vow there.[87] Christian writers also mentioned Onias and his temple, but with the exception of Eusebius and Jerome they seem to have had very little accurate knowledge of this distant episode. Yet Heliopolis itself did not lose its religious significance, for some Christians recounted how, during the Flight to Egypt (Matt 2:13-

---

[83] It is quite possible that the two coins of the second year of the Great Revolt found in Saqqarah (D.J. Thompson, *Memphis*, 270) were brought from Judea by the Jewish refugees themselves, or by the Roman soldiers who pursued them.
[84] See A. Fuks, "The Jewish Revolt," 144-5, and J. Mélèze Modrzejewski, *Les juifs d'Egypte*, 161-81. A.-P. Zivie "Onias," 570, follows N. Golb, "Topography," 140, in suggesting that the medieval Jewish community of Shibin-el-Qanatir included descendants of the Oniad settlers.
[85] See P.Harris 66 (155 CE); P.Lond. II, 317 (156 CE); P.Oxy. IV, 719 (193 CE), with U. Wilcken, *Grundzüge*, 1:53, and H. Braunert, *Binnenwanderung*, 128, 232. See also PGM IV.2441-55 (narrating an event of 130/1 CE?), P.Oxy. LX, 4060.97 (161 CE), P. Berol. inv. 6866.68 (172-192 CE; see J. Lesquier, *L'armée romaine*, 218), and the two Heliopolitan coins punlished by R.S. Poole, *Catalogue*, 344 (Antoninus Pius), and E. Christiansen, *Coins*, 120 (Marcus Aurelius).
[86] Jerome, *In Dan.*, III.XI.14: "neque urbis neque templi ullum restat vestigium."
[87] See m *Menahot* 13:10; t *Menahot* 13:12-5; b *Menahot* 109b; *Avoda Zara* 52b; *Megilla* 10a; p *Yoma* 6.3 (43d). For a plausible interpretation of the rabbis' geographical error, see A. Wasserstein, "Notes on the Temple of Onias."

5), the boy Jesus visited Heliopolis and performed a miracle there.[88] Such stories guaranteed the site a place of honor in Christian Egypt, and ωΝ-ʻΗλιόπολις (al-Matarieh, or Ein-Shams, in Arabic texts) remained a place of Coptic pilgrimage for many generations to come.[89] Onias' temple, however, is never mentioned in the accounts of Jesus' miracle, and we may only speculate whether the Coptic attachment to Heliopolis was somehow influenced by its Jewish past.[90] Regardless of such speculation, it can certainly be stated that Onias' temple has left no tangible mark on the groups which eventually emerged from the wreckage of the Jewish revolts, Rabbinic Judaism and the Christian Church. For them, the episode we have been reconstructing here is but a minor dead-end street in their long and tortuous histories. This, however, is something that Onias, Chelkias, and Ananias could never have imagined.

---

[88] W. Schneemelcher, *New Testament Apocrypha*, 1:460; E. Amélineau, *La géographie de l'Egypte*, 246-7.
[89] E. Amélineau, *La géographie de l'Egypte*, 287-8; M. Jullien, *L'Egypte*, 190-215; S. Timm, *Christlische-koptische Ägypten*, 910-4; 1613-20.
[90] Cf. A. Zivie, "Tell el Yahoudieh," 13-4.

Chapter 3

Joseph and Aseneth: Beyond the Honeycomb Scene

Our analysis of the central scene of *Joseph and Aseneth*, the angel's visit and his conversation with Aseneth, has shown it to contain a symbolic description of the establishment of Onias' Heliopolitan temple in the second century BCE. This new interpretation could pave the way for a reevaluation of the novel as a whole, and so our next move—having examined the history of Onias' temple—is to ask whether there are other sections or elements of *Joseph and Aseneth* which could support the suggestion of an Oniad provenance for the entire work.[1]

It is, of course, extremely difficult to contextualize a document about which little "external" information is available, and whose date and provenance must be deduced mainly from "internal" evidence. This is especially true for a work such as *Joseph and Aseneth*, which deliberately adopts an archaizing, biblical style, and carefully avoids any obvious anachronisms. In contextualizing such a narrative, arguments based on known historical events mentioned, or alluded to, in the story must always take precedence over arguments based on the author's perceived interests and *Weltanschauung*. But having noted the text's symbolic reference to the establishment of Onias' temple—apparently the only historical event alluded to in our story—we must now focus our attention on what can be deduced about the text's *Sitz im Leben* from other elements within the narrative. The best way to proceed is, once

---

[1] As will become clear throughout this and the following chapters, I see no reason to divide *Joseph and Aseneth* into different "layers" or "sources," as do, e.g., L.M. Wills, *The Jewish Novel*, 158-84, and J.C. O'Neil, "What is *Joseph and Aseneth*."

again, to look at one piece of evidence at a time. Only detailed probes into specific narrative regions can give us the certainty that we are, indeed, on the right track.

3.1. Jews, Egyptians, and Pharaoh[2]

No reader of *Joseph and Aseneth* can fail to note the author's disdain for Egyptians. This attitude finds its clearest expression when Joseph is welcomed by his host:

> And Joseph entered Pentephres' house and sat upon the throne. And they washed his feet and set aside a separate table for him, because Joseph did not eat with the Egyptians, for he found it detestable (βδέλυγμα ἦν αὐτῷ τοῦτο) (7:1).

This rude behavior toward one's hosts is, of course, an inversion of what we find in the biblical story, where we are explicitly told that it was *the Egyptians* who refused to eat with the Jews (Gen 43:32).[3] Our author clearly was embarrassed by this biblical statement, and chose to reverse it. But there might be more here than first meets the eye, for in a private letter, paleographically datable to the first century BCE, we hear that a certain Tebtunis priest would have to be taken care of during his stay in Memphis, "for you know that they detest Jews" (οἶδας γὰρ ὅτι βδελύσ⟨σ⟩ονται Ἰουδαίους).[4] The appearance here of the very same verb, βδελύσσω, is, of course, accidental, but it does seem that Joseph's behavior is a reversal not only of the biblical narrative, where it is the Egyptians who detest the Jews, but of what the author may have known from his own days—that his next-door neighbors in Memphis detest them too!

Our author's dislike for Egyptians, however, is not limited to this insistence on dietary segregation. It permeates even the description of his main protagonist, Aseneth:

---

[2] In a way, the following section merely expands on what Momigliano noted long ago, when briefly discussing *Joseph and Aseneth*: "[Its] whole atmosphere is that of the second or first century B.C., when the Jews felt well rooted and powerful in the land of Egypt" (*Alien Wisdom*, 118). Cf. S. West, "Joseph and Asenath," 80-1.

[3] Cf. also Gen 46:34, on the Egyptians' disgust with shepherds, undoubtedly implied in Aseneth's derogatory remark that Joseph is just "a shepherd's son from the land of Canaan" (4:10; cf. 6:2).

[4] See CPJ I, 141, with R. Rémondon, "Les Antisémites de Memphis," 244-61.

> She was in no way like the Egyptian virgins, but was in every respect
> like the daughters of the Hebrews; and she was tall like Sarah and
> handsome like Rebecca and beautiful like Rachel (1:5).

Apparently, Egyptian women impressed our author as greatly inferior
to the daughters of the Hebrews, and so he sought to stress that Aseneth
was an exception to the rule—as pretty as a Jewish girl, even as pretty
as the Matriarchs themselves. And yet, she was an Egyptian girl nonetheless, worshipping those "dumb and dead idols," eating their "bread
of strangulation," drinking their "cup of treachery," and anointing
herself with their "ointment of destruction" (8:5; 21:14; cf. 11:8-9, 16;
12:5). Only after meeting Joseph did she come to realize her error and
repent:

> Behold all the gods whom I once had worshipped in ignorance—I
> realized that they are dumb and dead idols, and I let them be
> trampled upon by men, and the thieves grabbed the ones that were
> made of silver and gold (13:11).[5]

There is, of course, nothing unique about *Joseph and Aseneth's*
negative assessment of the "idol-maniac" (12:9) Egyptians, for it finds
ample parallels in numerous passages in the Hebrew Bible and in post-
biblical Jewish literature. Egypt, the land of idolatry *par excellence*, was
a favorite target of pious Jewish polemics ever since the days of the
Prophets, and throughout the Greco-Roman period. In this, at least,
Joseph and Aseneth is not alone.[6]

What is more surprising, however, is the marked contrast between
our author's negative assessment of Egyptians and his favorable
attitude to the Egyptian king, Pharaoh, displayed throughout the novel.
Thus, when Joseph finally agrees to marry Aseneth, after her repentance
and following the angel's approval, he refuses to accept her father's
offer that he, Pentephres, will arrange everything. No, Joseph insists,

---

[5] Cf. the reference (10:13; 13:8) to the "strange dogs," who ate Aseneth's discarded
sacrifices, which has been construed as a joke aimed at Egyptian zoolatry, with the
"gods" eating their sacrifices (D. Sänger, "Bekehrung und Exodus," 20)—but note
Tabubu's similar action in M. Lichtheim, *Ancient Egyptian Literature*, 3:135.
[6] See Isa 19; Jer 46:13-26 etc.; *Let. Arist.* 138; *Sib. Or.* III.29-35; Philo, *Vita Mosis*
II.162; *Dec.* 76-9; *Vita Cont.* 8-9; *Ebr.* 95; *Leg. ad Gaium* 139, 163. See also Josephus'
unflattering characterization of the Egyptian nation in *Ant.* II.201, and G. Bohak,
"The Ibis and the Jewish Question."

> I will go tomorrow to king Pharaoh, for he is like my father (ὡς πατήρ μου), and he appointed me chief of the whole land of Egypt, and I will speak to him about Aseneth, and he himself will give her to me as my wife (20:9).

To hear Joseph, "the (firstborn) son of God" (6:3 etc.), saying that the Egyptian king is "like (his) father," is quite surprising, but when Joseph goes to Pharaoh,

> Pharaoh was very glad, and said to Joseph, "But isn't she betrothed to you since eternity? And she shall be your wife from now on and forever" (21:3).

Apparently, Pharaoh too has heard that this marriage is "since eternity" (15:10) and "forever" (15:6, 9). He sends for Pentephres and his daughter, who promptly arrive,

> and Pharaoh saw Aseneth and was amazed at her beauty and said, "The Lord, the God of Joseph, will bless you, child, and this beauty of yours will remain forever, for the Lord, the God of Joseph, rightly has chosen you as a bride for Joseph, because he is the firstborn son of God, and you shall be called a daughter of the Most High and a bride of Joseph from now on and forever." (21:4).

Once again, it seems that Pharaoh knows about Joseph, Aseneth, and God's plans for both more than any other figure in our novel, except for Levi (see below) and the angel himself. Moreover, to hear an Egyptian king calling Joseph's God "the Lord" and "the Most High," one would think that he too is about to repent his idolatry and worship the Jewish God, an impression which is only strengthened in the subsequent passage:

> And Pharaoh took Joseph and Aseneth and placed golden crowns on their heads, crowns which had been in his house from the beginning of time. And Pharaoh placed Aseneth at Joseph's right side and put his hands on their heads, and his right hand was on Aseneth's head. And Pharaoh said, "The Lord God, the Most High, will bless you and multiply you and magnify and glorify you forever." (21:5-6).

Reading such a description, we must note Pharaoh's great piety, quite unexpected of an Egyptian king, and his confident assertion that "the Lord God, the Most High" approves of Joseph and Aseneth's wedding

and will bless them eternally. We must also note the author's insistence
that it was Pharaoh himself who conducted every stage of the ceremony,
from the young couple's first kiss (21:7) to the grand banquet which
followed:

> And afterward Pharaoh gave a wedding feast and a great banquet
> and much drinking for seven days. And he summoned all the chiefs
> of the land of Egypt and all the kings of the nations and proclaimed
> in the whole land of Egypt that, "Any man who works during the
> seven days of the wedding of Joseph and Aseneth shall surely die"
> (21:8).

Joseph's wedding—the same Joseph who refused to eat with
Egyptians because "he found it detestable" (7:1)—consists of a great
banquet for all the Egyptian grandees and the kings of all other nations,
a banquet hosted by Pharaoh himself. What's more, the whole of Egypt
must cease work for seven days, to celebrate the wedding of this
"shepherd's son from the land of Canaan," as Aseneth once called him
(4:10), and the daughter of the high priest of Heliopolis. Needless to say,
our author did not derive these details from the Bible's terse statement
that "Pharaoh… gave him Aseneth, Daughter of Potiphera, the priest of
On, as his bride" (Gen 41:45), nor were they necessitated by some
hermeneutic difficulty with that biblical verse. If they appear in *Joseph
and Aseneth*, it is because the author sought to stress that this wedding
won Pharaoh's complete approval, and was witnessed by all the
grandees of Egypt and by the kings of all other nations. In fact, his desire
to emphasize this aspect of the wedding outweighed even his own wish
to depict Joseph as scrupulously avoiding excessive social contact with
the idolatrous Egyptians.

Our author's favorable assessment of Pharaoh is also evident in
the final section of the novel. Having killed some 2,050 enemy soldiers,[7]
the good brothers have won the fight, and Benjamin wants to do away
with Pharaoh's son himself. But Levi prevents this (in a scene we shall
return to below), and does his best to heal the bleeding prince "for if he
lives, he shall be our friend afterward, and his father Pharaoh shall be
like our father (ὡς πατὴρ ἡμῶν)" (29:4). He brings the prince to Pharaoh,
who is highly impressed, immediately prostrating himself before Levi
(29:6). Although the prince dies three days later (29:7), Joseph retains his
most-favored status in Pharaoh's court:

---

[7] Fifty mounted archers in 27:2-5 and 2,000 soldiers in 27:6.

> And Pharaoh mourned his firstborn son very much, and from his mourning he became very weak. And Pharaoh died at the age of one hundred and nine years, and he left his diadem to Joseph. And Joseph reigned in Egypt for forty-eight years, and afterward he handed the diadem to Pharaoh's younger son, who was still at the breast when Pharaoh died. And Joseph was like a father (ὡς πατήρ) to Pharaoh's younger son in the land of Egypt all the days of his life (29:8-9).

In these verses, which end our novel, we see Joseph, who had described Pharaoh as being like his father (20:9 cf. 24:14), treating Pharaoh's son as his own, thus becoming, in fact, part of the royal family itself. In the process, he even reigns over Egypt for forty-eight years—yet another detail which is never mentioned, or even hinted at, in the biblical Joseph-story. Once again, there can be little doubt as to the high esteem which our author had for Pharaoh and his house, and to the close cooperation between that house and Egypt's Jews which he envisioned.

Our author's dislike of Egyptians on the one hand and admiration for Pharaoh on the other may serve as useful clues in our quest for the origins of *Joseph and Aseneth*. First, his attitude toward Pharaoh certainly points to the Ptolemaic period, and not to Roman times—when Egypt was ruled, "loco regum," by Roman prefects,[8] and the "Pharaoh" himself was far away, and had no Jewish courtiers—as the time in which our novel must have been written. Second, they probably point to Jewish circles which depended on the friendship and protection of the Ptolemaic court, and so depicted their own forefathers as intimately connected with the Pharaonic court—far more intimately than even a reader of the biblical Joseph-story would have imagined.

Neither of these features is, of course, unique to *Joseph and Aseneth* alone—the *Letter of Aristeas* immediately comes to mind—and their centrality in our novel does not necessitate postulating an Oniad origin for our novel. Yet both features would fit extremely well within such an historical context. Assuming *Joseph and Aseneth* to have been written by one of Onias' supporters certainly would explain the novel's anti-Egyptian slant—a mirror-image, as it were, of what some Egyptians were saying about Onias' Heliopolitan settlement and about Jews in general.[9] Moreover, this assumption would also explain the

---

[8] Tacitus, *Hist.* I.11.1; cf. Strabo, *Geog.* XVII.1.12.
[9] Cf. G. Bohak, "CPJ III, 520," and Chapter 6.4, below.

author's strong emphasis on royal patronage and on seeking, and receiving, the king's ungrudging approval. After all, it was Onias' relations with Ptolemy VI Philometor which assured his own success, and it was the king's permission which enabled him to build his Heliopolitan temple and to control the territory around it.

3.2. The Patriarchs as Soldiers

The issue to which we now turn is our author's interest in military affairs, especially visible in the detailed battle descriptions dispersed throughout the last third of the novel (chapters 23-9). The most telling example is the elaborate tactical plan which two of the wicked brothers, Dan and Gad, present to Pharaoh's son:

> And Dan and Gad said to him, "We are your slaves today, and we will do everything that you have ordered us. We will go at night and lay an ambush in the wadi, and hide in the thicket of reeds. And you, take with you fifty mounted archers, and go before us, far ahead. And Aseneth will come and fall into our hands, and we will cut down the men who are with her, and she will flee ahead with her carriage and fall into your hands, and you will do to her as your soul desires." (24:19).

This two-stage military maneuver wins the approval of Pharaoh's son, who supplies the wicked brothers with 2,000 men. The ambush is laid out (24:20), and all is ready for the showdown. At first, everything proceeds smoothly. At daybreak, Aseneth leaves home and passes through the wadi, escorted by 600 men,

> and suddenly those who lay in ambush sprang up and joined battle with Aseneth's men and cut them down by the sword and killed all her forerunners. And Aseneth fled ahead with her carriage (26:5).

Stage one of the ambush is a great success, and stage two immediately follows. Pharaoh's son, with his fifty mounted archers, blocks Aseneth's way (26:7) and is about to capture her. But seeing the enemy's cavalry, Aseneth invokes the name of the Lord (26:8), while Benjamin collects stones and hurls them at the approaching force. With one stone he wounds Pharaoh's son, and with fifty others he kills as many mounted archers (27:1-5). Yet even this is not the end of the battle, for the four wicked brothers are still there to be reckoned with, and they approach

Aseneth with their swords drawn, ready for the kill (27:7-9). She is terrified and prays to God, reminding Him how He had saved her from the idols and promised her soul eternal life (27:10). Her prayer is heeded, the enemies' swords turn to ashes (27:11), and they quickly surrender (28:1-2).

This entire section of *Joseph and Aseneth*, with its elaborate maneuvers and detailed battle scenes, could have been summarized in five short sentences. The fact that it does get so much space in the narrative might tell us something about the author's own interests.[10] Moreover, although this military interest finds ample parallels in other Greek novels,[11] it has exceptional significance here, for the author, an Egyptian Jew, focusses not on some historically insignificant figures—as the Greek novels often do—but on his own forefathers.[12] It is his distant ancestors whom he describes as military experts, quick and mighty with their swords, which "shine forth like a flame of fire," and inspire fear even in the prince's bold heart (23:15). As noted by Collins, "The armed prowess of Levi and Simeon recalls the heyday of Jewish mercenaries in Egypt, which virtually disappeared after the Roman conquest."[13] Yet this is not only a chronological clue—pointing once again to the Ptolemaic period as the most natural time-frame for *Joseph and Aseneth*'s composition—but a sociological one as well. It cannot, of course, prove the novel's Oniad origins, for there were many Jewish soldiers in Ptolemaic Egypt. However, attributing the text to the largest group of such soldiers, those settled in and around Heliopolis, certainly would provide the most natural context within which to interpret this aspect of our novel.

3.3. Levi

One aspect of *Joseph and Aseneth* which has not received the attention it deserves is the author's admiring treatment of Levi, who is in some

---

10 The author's military background might also be evident from two interesting metaphors: in 18:9, Aseneth's teeth are compared to "soldiers lined up for battle," and in 22:9, Aseneth hugs Jacob "like someone hanging on his father's neck when he returns home from war." In both cases, however, the text is uncertain—cf. Ch. Burchard, "Ein vorläufiger griechischer Text," nn. 24 and 63, respectively.
11 See, e.g., A. Scarcella, "La polémologie des romans."
12 Cf. M. Braun, *History and Romance*, 1-6.
13 J.J. Collins, *Between Athens and Jerusalem*, 91.

ways superior even to Aseneth and Joseph themselves. This is evident already from Levi's first appearance in our novel, following Joseph's visit to his father, Jacob, to introduce his new wife. The newly-weds begin their journey home,

> but only Simeon and Levi, Joseph's brothers, the sons of Leah, escorted them... And Levi was on Aseneth's right side and Joseph on her left, and Aseneth held Levi's hand. And Aseneth loved Levi much more than all of Joseph's brothers, because he was attached to the Lord (ἦν προσκείμενος πρὸς τὸν κύριον), and he was a wise man (ἀνὴρ συνίων) and a prophet of the Most High (προφήτης ὑψίστου) and sharp-sighted with his eyes, and he saw letters written in heaven by the finger of God (γράμματα γεγραμμένα ἐν τῷ οὐρανῷ τῷ δακτύλῳ τοῦ θεοῦ),[14] and he knew the unspeakable (mysteries) of the Most High God and secretly revealed them to Aseneth (καὶ ᾔδει τὰ ἄρρητα θεοῦ τοῦ ὑψίστου καὶ ἀπεκάλυπτεν αὐτὰ τῇ Ἀσενὲθ κρυφῇ), for Levi loved Aseneth very much, and he saw her place of rest in the highest, and her walls like adamantine eternal walls, and her foundations founded upon a rock of the seventh heaven (22:11-3).

Three points are emphasized in this passage: Levi's attachment to the Lord, his supernatural abilities, and his close relationship with Aseneth. The first quality is, of course, based on an etymology of Levi's Hebrew name, לוי (לוה, "to accompany, be attached to"). This etymology has its origins in the Hebrew Bible, where Levi's descendants are said to be "attached to" Aaron and to accompany him in his priestly services (Num 18:2, 4). In post-biblical literature, it undergoes a further development, namely, that Levi "was attached" to the Lord himself (cf. *Jub* 31:16). Our author was familiar with, and utilized, a similar tradition, although the pun itself is entirely lost when rendered in Greek (Λευί... προσκείμενος).

While Levi's "attachment" to the Lord is readily explicable and well documented, his two other characteristics—his prophetic nature and especially his love for Aseneth—are less familiar, and all the more intriguing since they are stressed again and again in the final section of *Joseph and Aseneth*. When Pharaoh's son tries to enlist Simeon and Levi in his evil plot, for example, we learn that Simeon, "a daring and bold man," is infuriated with the young prince and wishes to kill him (23:7),

> but Levi saw his heart's desire, for Levi was a prophet (ἀνὴρ προφήτης), and he was sharp-sighted with his mind and eyes, and he

---

[14] For reading such heavenly texts, see, e.g. *1 Enoch* 103:2; 106;19; *Jub.* 32:21; cf. G. Delling, "Einwirkungen," 49.

could read what is written in men's hearts. And Levi trod with his foot on Simeon's right foot and pressed it and signaled to him to cease from his wrath. And Levi said to Simeon quietly, "Why are you furious with this man? For we are pious men (ἄνδρες θεοσεβεῖς), and it does not befit us to repay evil for evil" (23:8-9).

Levi now turns to Pharaoh's son, telling him that Simeon and he are "pious men," that their father is "a friend of the Most High God," and that their brother Joseph "is like the firstborn son of God" (23:10). No, they will never hurt their brother, for "it does not befit a pious man to harm any man in any way" (23:12).

Levi, then, is not merely a prophet, who can read even "what is written in men's hearts," but also a pious man who does not repay evil for evil, and would not betray his beloved brother, Joseph, under any circumstances. In a subsequent scene, when Aseneth is almost caught by Pharaoh's son, it is Levi's prophetic ability which is so instrumental in saving her:

And Levi, like a prophet (ὡς προφήτης), perceived it all and told his brothers, the sons of Leah, of Aseneth's predicament. And they all took their swords... and pursued after Aseneth in full haste (26:6).

This quick intervention saves the day, and the wicked plot crumbles. Dan, Gad, Naphthali, and Asher now fear for their lives, and beg Aseneth's forgiveness (28:1-6). She calms their fear, and tells them to hide in the thicket of reeds until things cool down a bit (28:7). Soon, Leah's sons arrive on the scene, "seeking their brothers... in order to kill them" (28:9). Simeon, that "daring and bold man," argues with Aseneth, who tries in vain to appease him (28:12-4), and Levi's omniscience and benevolence are put to good use once again:

And Levi went to Aseneth and kissed her right hand. And he knew that she wanted to save the men from their brothers' wrath so that they would not kill them. And they were nearby in the thicket of reeds, and Levi, their brother, knew it, but did not tell his brothers, for he was afraid lest in their wrath they would cut them down (28:15-7).

Levi's kind and forgiving nature is also apparent in the final scene (29:1-6), when he saves Pharaoh's son from death at the hands of Benjamin. Having shot a stone right through the prince's left temple (27:2), Benjamin wants to finish the job. He takes the prince's sword, "because

Benjamin did not have a sword on his thigh," and prepares for the final strike (29:2),

> but Levi ran up to him and held his hand and said, "Don't do this, brother, for we are pious men (ἄνδρες θεοσεβεῖς), and it does not befit a pious man to repay evil for evil nor to trample upon a fallen enemy nor to oppress him to death. And now, return your sword to its place, and come, help me, and we will heal him of his wound; and if he lives, he will be our friend afterward, and his father, Pharaoh, will be like our father." And Levi raised Pharaoh's son off the ground and washed the blood off his face and tied a bandage to his wound and put him on his horse and brought him to his father, Pharaoh, and told him everything. And Pharaoh rose from his throne and prostrated himself before Levi on the ground and blessed him (29:3-6).

This is a remarkable scene. All that Benjamin wished to do was to take the prince's sword and cut his head off—just as David would do to Goliath many years later (1 Sam 17:49-51)—but Levi does not allow this. Levi, we learn once again, is a man of the highest moral integrity, the paragon of the pious man.[15] Even Pharaoh acknowledges this, and prostrates himself before our hero, this obscure immigrant from Judea whose moral rectitude the great king finds so impressive.

Throughout *Joseph and Aseneth*, then, Levi is depicted as a prophetic visionary, Aseneth's best friend, and an extremely kind and pious person. Moreover, the two brothers whom we might have expected to be prominent in our narrative remain almost invisible. Neither Reuben, the eldest of the brothers, nor Judah, the eponymous father of the whole Jewish nation, have any role to play in our novel—in spite of their prominent roles in the biblical Joseph-story (Gen 37-50)—and both are mentioned only once (27:6).[16] It is Levi, and only Levi, who occupies center stage, together with Aseneth and Joseph, and sometimes outshining both.[17]

How are we to explain this phenomenon? It seems to me that the best explanation is that our author was himself a descendant of Levi, sharing his forefather's piety, his "attachment" to the Lord, and his

---

[15] For a possible motive for Levi's treatment of the wounded prince, cf. Josephus, *Ant.* IV.277.

[16] In fact, Judah's absence from our novel is so pronounced that it is Benjamin who is described as "a lion's whelp" (27:2; cf. Gen 49:9).

[17] Cf. also *Joseph and Aseneth*'s description of Levi with the negative assessment of Gen 49:5-7.

knowledge of "the unspeakable (mysteries) of the Most High God." He was, in other words, a Jewish priest, who was deeply interested in Levi, the primogenitor of the entire Jewish priesthood, elevated him above all of Jacob's other sons, and insisted that even Pharaoh had recognized his greatness.[18] Naturally, such a conclusion does not necessitate an Oniad origin for our novel, for there were Jewish priests in Greco-Roman Egypt even outside Heliopolis. Yet attributing it to that large priestly center certainly could provide a most suitable context for *Joseph and Aseneth*'s pronounced bias in Levi's favor.

3.4. Good Brothers, Bad Brothers

As is obvious from even a casual reading of *Joseph and Aseneth*, its final section (chapters 22-9) is devoted entirely to the feud between Pharaoh's son, aided by four of Joseph's brothers, and between Joseph, Aseneth, and Joseph's remaining brothers. We have already examined several aspects of this dispute, but it is now time to focus on its very core, namely, the familial conflict depicted by our author. This conflict among Joseph's brothers is all the more significant in light of the symbolic scenario depicted in the honeycomb scene, for the bad bees' attempt to hurt Aseneth (16:22-3) undoubtedly parallels the bad brothers' plot against her. In both cases, the forces of evil try to hurt Aseneth, fail, and soon are forgiven. Moreover, in both cases an inner-Jewish conflict is involved—that between good bees and bad ones, and that between Jacob's good and bad sons. Thus, it is safe to say that on the narrative level the events of the honeycomb scene foreshadow the internecine conflict of chapters 22-9, while on the historical level that conflict foreshadows the events depicted in the honeycomb scene—Onias' flight to Heliopolis, and the inner priestly conflicts that precipitated his move and were exacerbated by it.

Before assessing the historical significance of this conflict, however, we must focus on its literary manifestations. To begin with, we may note that while the conflict erupts only after the wicked prince's evil scheming, it must have been simmering under the surface for quite a while. When Joseph introduces Aseneth to his family, the young couple is warmly received by Jacob, Levi, Simeon, and Leah's other sons, but not

---

[18] For the glowing descriptions of Levi in other Jewish priestly texts, cf. J. Kugel, "Levi's Elevation," and D. Goodblatt, *The Monarchic Principle*, esp. 43-9.

3. Beyond the Honeycomb Scene

by the sons of Zilpah and Bilhah—Dan, Gad, Naphthali, and Asher—
who "envied them and hated them (ἐφθόνουν καὶ ἤχθραινον αὐτοῖς)"
(22:11). It is these feelings of jealousy and hatred which Pharaoh's well
informed son (24:2) subsequently utilizes, telling the disgruntled brothers
that he has heard Joseph plotting to kill them once Jacob passes away
(24:8). The prince also mentions Joseph's alleged statement that it had
been these same brothers who had sold him to the Ishmaelites many
years earlier (24:9). This statement—which is, of course, not based on
the biblical account of that event (Gen 37:25-8)—is later corroborated by
Naphthali and Asher, who state that Dan and Gad had sold Joseph
(25:5), and by Simeon, who alludes to that event yet again (28:13).

The fissure within Jacob's family, then, began long before
Aseneth's arrival on the scene, and is in no way caused by her presence
there.[19] Moreover, this fissure is not merely an old dispute between
jealous brothers, for there seems to be an enormous gap separating the
good brothers from the bad ones. This gap is most pronounced in *Joseph
and Aseneth's* description of the high moral standards expected of all
"pious men," and especially their refusal to repay evil for evil. When
Pharaoh's son tries to entice Simeon and Levi to join him in scheming
against their brother, Levi urges Simeon, as we have seen, to leave the
bold prince unharmed (23:9). He then turns to Pharaoh's son, patiently
explaining that Simeon and he would never join him, for "it does not
befit a pious man to harm any man in any way (οὐ προσήκει ἀνδρὶ
θεοσεβεῖ ἀδικεῖν πάντα ἄνθρωπον κατ᾽ οὐδένα τρόπον)" (23:12). Yet this
insistence on not repaying evil for evil is not shared by all of Jacob's
sons, for Dan, Gad, Naphthali, and Asher repeatedly ignore it. First,
they envy Joseph and Aseneth and hate them (22:11). Then, when
Pharaoh's son falsely alleges that he has overheard Joseph and Pharaoh
scheming against them, they readily take his word for it, and vow to join
him in his fight against Joseph (24:7-19). They are, in other words, eager
to repay evil even for an alleged, and unfounded, evil. Especially
noteworthy in this regard are Dan and Gad's cruel plan to "kill Joseph...
and kill his children before his very eyes" (24:19), and their refusal to
give up their wicked plan even when Naphthali and Asher have second
thoughts (25:5-7).

Dan, Gad, Naphthali, and Asher are well aware of the difference
between their brothers' behavior and their own. As they tell Aseneth,

---

[19] *Pace* R.D. Chesnutt, *From Death to Life*, 108-115.

once their scheme collapses, "we know that our brothers are pious men
(οἴδαμεν ὅτι οἱ ἀδελφοὶ ἡμῶν ἄνδρες εἰσὶ θεοσεβεῖς), and do not repay evil
for evil to any man" (28:5). She confirms their statement, saying that
they must not fear their brothers, "for they are pious men, and fear the
Lord (διότι αὐτοί εἰσιν ἄνδρες θεοσεβεῖς καὶ φοβούμενοι τὸν θεόν) and
respect every man" (28:7). She too, then, is aware of the distinction
between Jacob's sons who are pious and those who are not. By forgiving
the bad brothers she also proves—if proof were needed—that she too
belongs with the pious, and does not repay evil for evil. Thus, in spite of
Leah's sons' first inclination to kill the plotters (28:9, 12-3), Levi and
Aseneth intervene, and the wayward brothers go unharmed (28:10-7).

    We may now sum up what we have seen thus far. *Joseph and
Aseneth*'s narrative presents us with two distinct social groups. On the
one hand, there are the "pious men," comprised of born Jews and of
non-Jews who repent of their idolatry and share the highest moral
standard. Ranged against them are the forces of evil, comprised of Jews
and non-Jews who share a tendency toward treachery and cruelty.
These two groups are, by their very nature, bound to confront each
other—a confrontation which has little to do with the events narrated in
our novel, since it began at least as early as the selling of Joseph to the
Ishmaelites, if not earlier. Within each of these groups, of course, there
is further internal gradation, for Joseph, Levi, Aseneth, and Jacob
certainly are more pious than Simeon, with his excessive rashness (23:7-
9; 28:12-4), or Reuben and Judah, whose moral stance is never even
mentioned. Among the forces of evil, Dan, Gad, and Pharaoh's son
certainly are more wicked than Naphthali and Asher.

    There is, finally, one more point that must be noted with regard to
the social divisions apparent in *Joseph and Aseneth*, namely, the way in
which the "pious men" treat their adversaries during the inevitable
confrontation. For while these evil forces are comprised of Jews and
non-Jews alike, our author clearly suggests very different treatments of
evil Jews on the one hand and their non-Jewish partners on the other.
When fighting the prince's soldiers, Aseneth's supporters use swords
(26:6; 27:6) and stones (27:2-5), and clearly aim to kill. When fighting
their own brothers, however, no weapons are used—only Aseneth's
prayer, invoking God's help against these intimate enemies (27:10-1).
Against non-Jews, in other words, all is permissible, but when fighting
Jews, the "pious man" must rely solely on God's help. God, of course, is
on the good brothers' side, as even the bad brothers must admit (25:5-6;

28:1, 3, 10). Moreover, the ultimate goal in an internecine conflict is not to kill your brother at all, for, as Aseneth says to Simeon,

> Leave it to the Lord to punish their effrontery (τῷ κυρίῳ δώσεις ἐκδικῆσειν τὴν ὕβριν αὐτῶν), for they are your brothers, and the family (γένος) of your father, Israel... Grant them pardon (28:14).

Simon, then, must not punish his brothers, but leave such matters to God. And God, as Aseneth had heard even before her conversion, is "merciful and compassionate and patient and forgiving and gentle, and he does not count the error of a humbled person, and does not punish the sin of an oppressed person at the time of his oppression" (11:10). It is repentance, not revenge, that God seeks—and every pious Jew must seek it too, when dealing with a wayward brother. It is for this reason that the bees who tried to harm Aseneth were allowed to settle in Aseneth's garden—they were given a second chance (16:23).

Our author's complex view of his forefathers' social world, and his deep interest in brotherly feuds, are, of course, important clues in any attempt to locate his own social context, for their prominence in *Joseph and Aseneth*'s narrative suggests that they reflect events and trends of the author's own time.[20] What these events were, however, is an open question, at least until we consider the brotherly conflict's similarity to the one between the good bee-priests and the bad ones in the honeycomb scene itself. With this in mind, the connection between the literary feud of chapters 22-9 and the historical feuds within the Jewish priesthood in the 170s and 160s BCE becomes ever more likely.

3.5. Food-Drink-Ointment

In addition to the moral rectitude common to all "pious men," several rules of behavior seem to characterize them. The most important of these is first mentioned when Joseph insists that he cannot kiss Aseneth,

> for it does not befit a pious man, who blesses with his mouth the living God and eats blessed bread of life (ἄρτον εὐλογημένον ζωῆς)

---

[20] See also R.D. Chesnutt, *From Death to Life*, 108-9, with the previous note, and D. Sänger, "Erwägungen," whose own suggestion—that the brotherly conflict reflects events in Alexandria in the late-30s CE—is vitiated by the lack of any supporting evidence.

and drinks a blessed cup of immortality (ποτήριον εὐλογημένον ἀθανασίας) and is anointed with a blessed ointment of incorrupti- bility (χρίσματι εὐλογημένῳ ἀφθαρσίας), to kiss a strange woman, who blesses with her mouth dead and dumb idols and eats from their table bread of strangulation and drinks from their libation a cup of insidiousness and is anointed with an ointment of destruction" (8:5).

This combination of "bread of life," "a cup of immortality," and "an ointment of incorruptibility," appears several times in *Joseph and Aseneth*, and is probably its most studied—and least understood— element.[21] In this specific passage, the food-drink-ointment sequence serves to highlight the gulf separating Joseph from Aseneth, her actions being the exact opposite of his. Thus, we might be tempted to conclude that this sequence merely reflects the gap between those who worship God (the literal meaning of θεοσεβής, "pious") and those who worship idols (e.g., Aseneth's ἐσεβάσθην εἴδωλα in 12:5; cf. 2:3; 9:2, etc.). Joseph's subsequent prayer, however, implies that this is not the case, for he beseeches God to "bless this virgin and renew her by your spirit... and let her eat your bread of life (ἄρτον ζωῆς σου) and drink your cup of blessing (ποτήριον εὐλογίας σου); and count her among your people, whom you have chosen before all things came into being; and let her enter your rest, which you have prepared for your chosen ones, and live in your eternal life forever" (8:9). From this passage, the food-drink-ointment sequence emerges as intimately connected with "the chosen ones"—that group whom Aseneth symbolically joins—and the connection becomes even more evident as the honeycomb scene unfolds. First, the angel presents Aseneth with the mysterious honeycomb and tells her that "all those who attach themselves to the Lord God in repentance (οἱ προσ- κείμενοι τῷ θεῷ τῷ ὑψίστῳ ἐν ὀνόματι τῆς μετανοίας)" will eat from this comb, as well as "all the angels of God (οἱ ἄγγελοι τοῦ θεοῦ)," "all the chosen ones of God (οἱ ἐκλεκτοὶ τοῦ θεοῦ)," and "all the sons of the Most High (οἱ υἱοὶ τοῦ ὑψίστου)" (16:14). Next, he makes her eat from the comb, and then tells her that she just "ate bread of life, and drank a cup of immortality, and (was) anointed with an ointment of incorruptibility" (16:16; cf. 19:5). Clearly, these actions are not common to all Jews, but only to the group whom Aseneth joins. Moreover, the food-drink- ointment sequence is equated here with the symbolic act of eating from

21 See Ch. Burchard, "The Importance of Joseph and Aseneth," with an extensive bibliography, and R.D. Chesnutt, *From Death to Life*, 128-36.

the honeycomb-temple. Thus, the conclusion seems inevitable that this sequence is directly related to that temple, and probably represents the "holy" food and anointing characteristic of Jewish priests ever since First Temple times.[22]

Unfortunately, not much is known about the observance of these regulations among the priests serving in Onias' temple, but there is some evidence for the practice of anointing among the Jewish priests in Egypt, and perhaps even in Heliopolis itself. First, we know of "Aristobulus… of anointed priestly stock (ὄντι δὲ ἀπὸ τοῦ τῶν χριστῶν ἱερέων γένους)," the addressee of one of the festal letters which open 2 Maccabees (2 Macc 1:10). While we cannot tell in which temple, if any, Arisobulus had served, this passage clearly shows that Jewish priestly anointing was not unknown in Egypt in the second century BCE. A second source, however, might be even more relevant here, namely, the Sibyl's chastisement of Memphis for its rage against the Lord's "God-anointed children (ἐς ἐμοὺς παῖδας θεοχρίστους)" (Sib. Or. V.68). This has often been suspected as a Christian interpolation, but for no real reason.[23] Rather, it would be much more natural to assume that this passage, written after the destruction of both Jewish temples in the early 70s CE, refers to Memphis' hatred of the Jewish priests in neighboring Heliopolis—a hatred whose traces may be found in CPJ I, 141, CPJ III, 520, and elsewhere.[24] These "God-anointed" children of the Lord, in other words, were none other than the "sons of God" of our novel, anointed with "a blessed ointment of incorruptibility."

To sum up: The combination of holy food, holy drink, and ointment is best understood as referring to the ritual purity observed by Jewish priests, in this case the Jewish priests who served in Onias' temple. Of course, Joseph's, and Aseneth's, partaking of this sequence—and no one else, not even Levi, joins them in this—is but a foretaste, as it were, of the distant future, when the bee-priests will leave their honeycomb-temple and build a new one in Heliopolis. Moreover, our author seems unsure whether Aseneth, as a woman, should have been anointed at all.

---

[22] For "holy" food, see Schürer (rev.), History, 2:257-67. For anointing, see Exod 28:41; 29:7, 21; 30:30; 40:13-5; Lev 7:35-6; Schürer (rev.), History, 2:244-5. Cf. T. Levi 8:2-10; 2 Enoch 22:8-10; M. Himmelfarb, Tours of Heaven, 36-41.

[23] J. Geffcken, Komposition, 29; cf. H.C.O. Lancaster, "The Sibylline Oracles," 398. Note the Sibyl's use of similar compounds—e.g., ναὸς θεότευκτος (V.150), and λαὸς θεότευκτος (V.502).

[24] G. Bohak, "CPJ III, 520."

Thus, after describing himself as a "pious man" who shares the food-drink-ointment sequence (8:5), Joseph prays to God that Aseneth would join "the chosen ones," and that she too would partake of the "bread of life" and the "cup of blessing"—but not the ointment (8:9). It is only the angel who first insists that Aseneth will share the food-drink-ointment sequence in its entirety (15:5), and then claims that she indeed has done so (16:16)—the same angel who previously told her that her head was "like that of a young man (καὶ ἡ κεφαλή σου ὡς ἀνδρὸς νεανίσκου)" (15:1). Aseneth herself, however, seems unfazed by her quasi-male status, for in describing what had happened she twice refers to the bread and the cup, without even mentioning the ointment (19:5; 21:21). Apparently, *Joseph and Aseneth*'s readers would have known that the "ointment of incorruptibility" should be limited to active, male priests, and its application to Aseneth, therefore, was kept to a minimum.[25]

3.6. "The Wild Old Lion Is Pursuing Me"[26]

Following Aseneth's repentance, she asks God to save her before she is caught by those who pursue her (ῥῦσαί με πρὶν καταληφθῆναί με ὑπὸ τῶν καταδιωκόντων με, 12:7), and to rescue her as a father rescues a little child (12:8). She also explains why it is that she is so terrified, and it is on this explanation that we must now focus:

> For behold, the wild old lion is pursuing me (ὁ λέων ὁ ἄγριος ὁ παλαιὸς καταδιώκει με), because he is the father of the gods of the Egyptians (αὐτός ἐστι πατὴρ τῶν θεῶν τῶν Αἰγυπτίων) and his children are the gods of the idol-maniacs (τὰ τέκνα αὐτοῦ εἰσιν οἱ θεοὶ τῶν εἰδωλομανῶν). And I hated them, because they are the lion's children (ὅτι τέκνα τοῦ λέοντός εἰσι), and I threw them all away from me and destroyed them. And the lion, their father, is furious, and he pursues me. But you, Lord, rescue me from his hands, and from his mouth deliver me, lest he grab me like a lion, and tear me apart, and throw me into the flame of the fire (εἰς τὴν φλόγα τοῦ πυρός), and the fire will throw me into the storm, and the storm (καταιγίς) will wrap me up in darkness (ἐν σκότει) and throw me out into the

---

25 For another possible priestly element in the novel, see R.T. Beckwith, "The Solar Calendar of Joseph and Asenath." Unfortunately, the evidence adduced by Beckwith does not suffice to demonstrate that the novel indeed presupposes the solar calendar of *Jubillees* and the Qumran sectarian texts.

26 The following section develops a suggestion of M. Philonenko, *Joseph et Aséneth*, 171.

deep of the sea (εἰς τὸν βυθὸν τῆς θαλάσσης), and the big sea monster who is since eternity (τὸ κῆτος τὸ μέγα τὸ ἀπ' αἰῶνος) will swallow me, and I will be destroyed forever. Rescue me, Lord, before all these things come upon me (12:9-12).

This is quite an intriguing prayer, no doubt, and one's first impression is that Aseneth's agitated mental state, and her week-long fasting, are responsible for this psychedelic description of her predicament. Yet there must be some sense to her prayer, detailed and graphic as it is, and so several scholars have suggested that the "wild old lion" whom Aseneth fears is the Devil himself, sometimes described in Jewish and Christian writings as a dangerous, devouring lion.[27] This is, of course, a possible interpretation, but a far better explanation suggests itself once we listen carefully to Aseneth's own words and understand their context within the narrative.

The key to the identity of the "wild old lion" is Aseneth's reference to him as "the father of the gods of the Egyptians." In ancient Egypt, quite a few gods could be referred to as "father of (all) the gods,"[28] but coming from the mouth of a Heliopolitan maiden, there is no doubt that she has Atum-Re, the Sun-god, in mind. He, self-begotten, gave birth to the other gods of the Great Ennead of Heliopolis, and is often called, in Egyptian texts of all periods, "the father of all the gods."[29] That he is described by Aseneth as a "wild old lion" is hardly surprising, given the abundant evidence to Atum-Re's manifestation as a lion in Egyptian literature,[30] in Greco-Roman discussions of Egypt and its gods,[31] and on Greco-Egyptian magical gems.[32] Thus, there can be little doubt that Aseneth's prayer to God is to save her from the fury of Atum-Re, the Egyptian Sun-god, that wild old lion who fathered all those gods whom she had just destroyed (12:9; cf. 10:12-3).

---

[27] Thus, e.g., G. Delling, "Einwirkungen," 52; U. Fischer, Eschatologie, 114; Ch. Burchard, "Joseph and Aseneth," 221, note c2.
[28] E. Hornung, Conceptions of God, 147-9.
[29] B. Watterson, The Gods of Ancient Egypt, 49; L. Kákosy, "Atum," 550; W. Barta, "Re," 159. Especially noteworthy are the references in T.G. Allen, The Book of the Dead, 10 (Spell 8a); 15 (Spell 15i); 27 (Spell 17a); 178 (Spell 170) etc.
[30] See, e.g., T.G. Allen, The Book of the Dead, 55 (Spell 62b), and especially C. de Wit, Le rôle et le sense du lion, 138-47.
[31] Plutarch, Quaest. Conv. IV.5.2: τὸν λέοντα τῷ ἡλίῳ συνοικειοῦσιν (sc. Αἰγύπτιοι) etc.; Aelian, NA XII.7.20; Horapollo, Hierog. I.17; Macrobius, Saturn. I.21.16. Cf. E. Bernand, "Le culte du lion."
[32] C. Bonner, Studies, 150-3; cf. PGM III.511; IV.1667, etc.

Aseneth's fear of Re's revenge certainly is justified, given the many descriptions in Egyptian literature of the punishments meted out to those who rebel against him. This is especially true of the so-called "Livres," the New Kingdom books that describe the Sun's journey through the nether world. There, in Zandee's words, "those who have sinned against Re or Osiris on earth... have to expiate (their sins)... by hellish punishments."[33] Even the harrowing torments she envisions—including the fire, the darkness, and the devouring monster—find ample parallels in these Egyptian accounts of what it is that the victorious Re does to his vanquished enemies.[34] It would, of course, be difficult to demonstrate that *Joseph and Aseneth* borrowed any of these elements from Egyptian sources, especially given the existence of similar motifs within the Hebrew Bible itself.[35] Yet the accurate reference to Re's leonine manifestation, and the general tone of the passage as a whole, vividly demonstrate our author's familiarity with at least some aspects of Egyptian (Heliopolitan) theology.[36]

There is, however, more to this passage than an intriguing echo of Egyptian literature, for it seems that our author displays in this passage a remarkable, and unusual, degree of psychological understanding.[37] What we see here is a convert who has abandoned her ancestral gods and turned to a new one, but who is still apprehensive of the old gods' revenge. It is easy to understand Aseneth's fear and sympathize with her anguish, for just as her conversion got her in trouble with her family,[38] it also got her in trouble with a ferocious Egyptian god whose "children" she had just renounced, pulverized, and thrown out of her window.

---

33 J. Zandee, *Death as an Enemy*, 223.

34 See J. Zandee, *Death as an Enemy*, 133-42 (fire); 88-91 (darkness); 97-102, 192-7 (monsters); cf. E. Hornung, *The Valley of the Kings*, 152-64; M. Philonenko, *Joseph and Aséneth*, 172-3. For Demotic and Coptic accounts of the sinners' fate, see Zandee, *ibid.*, 297-342.

35 See esp. G. Delling, "Einwirkungen," 52-3.

36 Cf. M. Philonenko, *Joseph et Aséneth*, 59-60 and 167-8, for possible Egyptian (Heliopolitan) influences on the cosmogony of 12:2.

37 The only other passage in which *Joseph and Aseneth* shows any psychological subtlety is in the description of Aseneth's hesitation before turning to the Most High God for help (11:15-9).

38 Note, however, *Joseph and Aseneth*'s inconsistency on this point: in 11:4-5 and 12:12 Aseneth claims that her parents "hated (μεμισήκασι)" and "disowned (ἠρνήσαντο)" her because she had abandoned their gods, but later she seems to be on very good terms with them (e.g., 20:6-21:1).

Aseneth, a Heliopolitan maiden, knew well what punishments await her—unless, of course, her new God intervenes.

3.7. Ioakim, the King of Moab

One obscure figure, mentioned in *Joseph and Aseneth* only in passing at the beginning of the novel, is "Ioakim, the king of Moab," whose daughter the young Egyptian prince was to marry.

> And Pharaoh's firstborn son heard about Aseneth, and he kept begging his father to give her to him as his wife. And Pharaoh's firstborn son said to him, "Father, give me Aseneth, the daughter of Pentephres, the priest of Heliopolis, as my wife." And Pharaoh, his father, said to him, "Why do you, who are king of the whole land of Egypt, seek a wife who is beneath you? Behold, is not the daughter of the king of Moab, Ioakim (Ἰωακείμ), betrothed to you? And she is a queen, and very beautiful—take her as your wife!" (1:7-9).

Ioakim's brief appearance here is doubly strange. First, our author does not normally assign names to his extra-biblical characters—the evil prince is simply called "Pharaoh's firstborn son" (1:7 etc.), Aseneth's mother's name goes unmentioned (3:5 etc.), Aseneth's steward is called "her steward, in charge of her house" (18:2 etc.), and Aseneth's favorite maiden is only known to us as "her foster-sister" (10:4). All these figures remain nameless, while the king of Moab, and only he, is identified by name. Moreover—and this is the second mystery—the king of Moab receives a perfectly good Jewish name, Ioakim.

To date, no interpretation of Ioakim's unexpected name has ever been proposed.[39] It seems to me, however, that once we consider the possibility of an Oniad origin for *Joseph and Aseneth*, this problem finds a rather surprising solution. As noted in the previous chapter, it was Alcimus-Iakimos (*Ant.* XII.385) who served as high priest in Jerusalem from 162 to 159 BCE, a position which was Onias IV's rightful lot. Obviously, Onias' followers had good reasons to dislike this usurper, who held the high priesthood while Onias was living in Egypt, and it would not be strange if one of them added a small joke at Iakimos' expense into his novel. This is why the king of Moab, whose daughter Pharaoh's son should have married instead of seeking for Aseneth,

---

[39] Cf. Ch. Burchard, "Joseph and Aseneth," 203, note u.

receives such an unexpected name. While the evil prince was betrothed to Iakimos' daughter, Joseph was betrothed, "since eternity" (21:3 etc.), to the beautiful maiden from Heliopolis!

We have analyzed several sections of *Joseph and Aseneth* and concentrated on diverse themes (Jews, Egyptians, and Pharaoh; the Patriarchs as soldiers; good brothers, bad brothers; food-drink-ointment) and figures (Levi; "the wild old lion;" Ioakim) that could point to an Oniad-Heliopolitan origin for the work as a whole. By itself, each of these narrative elements is not unique to *Joseph and Aseneth*, and cannot be taken as proof of the text's Oniad origins. Yet all these disparate lines of evidence seem to converge at one specific point. For if the novel was written by a Jewish author who was closely related to the Ptolemaic court, was deeply interested in military affairs, esteemed Levi above all the other sons of Jacob, paid much attention to issues of inner-Jewish strife, described "the chosen ones" as partaking of the priestly food and ointment, knew something about Heliopolitan mythology, and introduced a "Ioakim" into his narrative, it seems most likely that this authr was intimately connected with Onias' temple. Coming on top of the honeycomb scene, where the establishment of that temple is depicted in a symbolic vision, such evidence becomes all the more conclusive.

Chapter 4

The Oniad Topography of Heliopolis

In the previous chapter, our aim was to look for elements in *Joseph and Aseneth*, outside the honeycomb scene, that could support the suggestion of an Oniad provenance for the novel. The present chapter will focus on narrative elements that could be construed as serving the needs of the Oniad community in Heliopolis. This is, of course, a more speculative endeavor, for our understanding of the meaning which any narrative element might have had for its readers depends first and foremost on whom we imagine these readers to have been. Thus, in the current chapter we will assume an Oniad readership for our novel, and try to assess what such readers could have derived from various sections of *Joseph and Aseneth*. We will focus our attention on the city of Heliopolis—the site where *Joseph and Aseneth*'s entire plot takes place, and where we now assume the novel itself to have been written.

At first sight, it might seem as if our author has little to say about ancient Heliopolis, ignoring as he does even its famous obelisks and temples. Yet this hardly is surprising, given his attempt to set his story in the biblical past and write an appendix, as it were, to the biblical Joseph-story. In such a text, any obvious anachronism, and any reference to contemporary Heliopolis, would have disclosed the author's identity and damaged the story's credibility. Thus, even some typically Egyptian elements of the story are not specifically Heliopolitan. The "thicket of reeds (ἡ ὕλη τοῦ καλάμου)," for example, where the prince's supporters lay their ambush (24:19 etc.), is one of those Egyptian papyrus-marshes where ambuscading robbers often await their helpless prey,[1] but is in no way particular to the Heliopolitan region itself.

Yet while he ignores the city of Heliopolis, two specific locations do seem to attract the author's attention—the "field of inheritance" and Aseneth's tower. The present chapter will, therefore, be devoted to a close examination of these two landmarks.

4.1. "The Field of Our Inheritance"

The first topographic site which calls for a detailed examination is "the field of (their/our) inheritance." It first appears quite early in the novel:

> And Aseneth heard that her father and mother had come from the field of their inheritance (ἐξ ἀγροῦ τῆς κληρονομίας αὐτῶν), and she rejoiced and said, "I will go to see my father and my mother because they have come from the field of our inheritance (ἐξ ἀγροῦ τῆς κληρονομίας ἡμῶν)" (3:5).

This field must have been quite large, and very fertile, as becomes evident when her parents return:

> And they brought out all the good things which they had brought from the field of their inheritance, and gave them to their daughter. And Aseneth rejoiced over all the good things—the fruit (τ ῇ ὀπώρᾳ), the grapes (τῇ σταφυλῇ), the dates (τοῖς φοίνιξι), the doves (ταῖς περιστεραῖς),[2] the pomegranates (ταῖς ῥοαῖς), and the figs (τοῖς σύκοις)—for they were all handsome and good to taste (4:2).

All the delicious produce which grows in this "field of inheritance"—note the echoes of Gen 2:9 (the Garden of Eden) and Deut 8:8 (the Promised Land)—gives us the impression that our author thinks very highly of this field.[3] In fact, the field's productivity is quite supernatural, since this part of the story takes place in "the time of harvest" (ὥρα θερισμοῦ, 2:11; 3:5), which in Egypt would fall between April and June, while the description of the produce would make us think that it was

---

[1] Heliodorus, *Aethiopica* I.6 (cf. I.30, VIII.16); Achilles Tatius, *LC* IV.12; but note also Polybius III.71, for a similar scene outside Egypt.

[2] The περιστεραί seem a bit out of place here, and might be due to a textual corruption, although dove-cots were as familiar in ancient Egypt as they are today (see, e.g., P.G.P. Meyboom, *The Nile Mosaic*, 40, and fig. 27).

[3] Cf. the description of Judea's fertility in *Let. Arist.* 112.

already August or September (vintage time), or even October (date-picking time)![4] This obvious inconsistency is probably due to the author's perception of the wonderful fertility of this "field of inheritance," which, like the trees of Aseneth's garden (2:11), seems to be highly productive.

Yet this is not the last mention of the field in our story, for we later hear that Mr. and Mrs. Pentephres go there again (10:1), returning home only after the angel's visit (20:6). During that visit, the angel asks Aseneth, in a scene we already analyzed, to bring him a honeycomb, and she immediately says:

> I will send a slave-boy to the suburb, because the field of our inheritance is near, and he will quickly bring you a honeycomb from there, and I will serve it to you, Lord (16:4).

Apparently, honey too is produced in this wonderful field (cf. Dt 8:8), that lies within easy walking distance from Aseneth's house. Moreover, it seems that once Joseph has married Aseneth, the field is their inheritance, as is implied by Dan's and Gad's statement in 24:15, and by Aseneth's own words to Joseph, "I will go, just like you have said, to the field of our inheritance (εἰς τὸν ἀγρὸν τῆς κληρονομίας ἡμῶν)" (26:1). The field, which previously belonged to Aseneth's parents, now belongs to Joseph and her.[5]

Unfortunately, *Joseph and Aseneth* never mentions how the field had become Pentephres' own "inheritance," but this can be deduced from another section in the novel. When Pharaoh's son tries to enlist Simeon and Levi, he promises them great rewards in return for their support:

> I will take you today as my companions (ἑταίρους), and give you much gold and silver, and servants and maids and houses and big inheritances (κληρονομίας μεγάλας)... and you will become my brothers (ἀδελφούς) and faithful friends (φίλους πιστούς) (23:3-4).[6]

When Simeon and Levi refuse this generous offer, the prince turns to Gad, Dan, Naphthali, and Asher with a similar offer—if they join him, he would make them his "brothers (ἀδελφοί)" and "fellow-heirs of all his

---

[4] For Egypt's agricultural calendar, see, e.g., N. Lewis, *Life in Egypt*, 115-6.
[5] *Joseph and Aseneth* also mentions in passing that Aseneth's younger brother had died several years earlier (10:8). Was this seemingly irrelevant detail meant to assure the reader that Aseneth was the sole inheritor of her father's estate?
[6] For the prince's own lands, see also 25:2.

possessions" ⟨συγκληρονόμοι τῶν ἐμῶν πάντων⟩" (24:14)—to which they gladly agree. What we see in both passages is, of course, the typical Hellenistic practice of granting royal land to those who have rendered some service to the king or the state. In fact, even some of the terms used here—such as φίλοι and ἀδελφοί—find ample parallels in Ptolemaic documents.[7]

The prince's offers to Joseph's brothers clearly demonstrate how Pentephres himself might have aquired his "field of inheritance." Being Pharaoh's "advisor" and "chief of all his satraps and noblemen," one who was "more intelligent than all of Pharaoh's noblemen" (1:3), he must have received large tracts of land as a sign of royal gratitude. Yet this does not explain why our author found this field so important as to mention it again and again in his narrative, and why he was so persistent in describing its wonderful productivity, and in assuring his readers that it later passed to Aseneth and to her husband Joseph and became their own "field of inheritance." Certainly, neither the biblical Joseph-story nor *Joseph and Aseneth's* romantic plot necessitated such emphasis on agrarian issues.

If our author, and his intended readers, were Heliopolitan Jews, this lively interest in Aseneth's field is readily understandable. As noted above (Chapter 2.1.3), Onias received large tracts of land from Ptolemy VI Philometor, in an area which became known as "the Land of Onias," and seems to have been set aside for Jewish settlement. What we now learn is that there was full historical justification for this acquisition, for the territory around Heliopolis had once belonged to Pentephres, and through his daughter Aseneth it became Joseph's "field of inheritance." Onias and his followers, then, were not receiving Egyptian land from a Ptolemaic king, but reclaiming their ancestors' territories!

There are, of course, many Greco-Roman parallels to the use of existing ancient texts—or the fabrication of new ones—to support the territorial claims of this or that group.[8] To see how such claims could be made, we may look at one example, namely, Simeon's (the Hasmonean)

---

[7] For φίλοι, see the long list in L. Mooren, *Aulic Titulature*, 52-74; ἀδελφός is less common—συγγενής is the common title for such a person—but cf. OGIS 138; 168 etc., and the Demotic title "brother of the king" in Mooren, *ibid.*, 117; 120-2 etc. See further below, Chapter 6.2.
[8] For numerous examples—from *Jub.* 10:27-34 to the territorial implications of the Homeric Catalogue of Ships—see J.H. Levy, *Studies*, 60-78. Cf. also Polybius XVIII.51.3-6; OGIS 13; Heliodorus, *Aethiopica* VIII.1, etc., and below, Chapter 6.5.

explanation of why he had conquered Joppa, Gazara, and the citadel of Jerusalem and expelled their non-Jewish inhabitants:

> We have taken neither foreign land (γῆν ἀλλοτρίαν) nor foreign property, but the inheritance of our fathers (τῆς κληρονομίας τῶν πατέρων ἡμῶν), which at one time had been unjustly (ἀκρίτως) taken by our enemies. We have seized the opportunity and reclaimed our fathers' inheritance (ἀντεχόμεθα τῆς κληρονομίας τῶν πατέρων ἡμῶν) (1 Macc 15:33-4).

Simeon's words in justifying his military conquests form a close parallel to what the Oniad settlers may have done. To justify their settlement in the Heliopolite nome, they claimed that this territory had been their forefathers' "inheritance" ever since Joseph's marriage with Aseneth. This does not mean, of course, that Onias, or any of his followers, used *Joseph and Aseneth* as a basis for their territorial claims. Just like Simeon—who first conquered the territory and then came up with the historical justification, as convincing as he could make it to be[9]—the Oniad Jews first received the land from Philometor and then came up with the historical "facts" which could justify their action.

4.2. Aseneth's House

A second Heliopolitan landmark that looms large in *Joseph and Aseneth* is Aseneth's house, which is described in great detail at the beginning of the novel and plays a part in the subsequent narrative. It seems, moreover, that this is not only an ordinary house, but a temple as well— an impression which emerges from many small, but telling, details.

4.2.1. The Court, the Stream, and the Garden

At the very beginning of the novel (2:1-12), we learn that "Pentephres had a tower next to his house, very big and high" (2:1) set apart for Aseneth, and that there was a large court surrounding his house and her tower.

---

[9] Jerusalem and Gazara may indeed have been the Jews' "inheritance" (1 Ki. 9:16 etc.)—but Joppa certainly was not (Josh 19:46)!

> And there was a very high wall around the court, built from large square stones. And the court had four iron-plated gates, each guarded by eighteen strong young men bearing arms. And planted inside the court, along the wall, were handsome trees of all sorts and all bearing fruit. And their fruit was ripe, for it was the time of harvest. And in the court, on the right hand, was a spring of abundant living water, and below the spring was a big cistern receiving the water of that spring. And a stream ran from there, through the court, and watered all the trees of that court (2:10-2).

The complex described here is of a type well known to students of ancient Egypt. There is no mistaking its resemblance to Tabubu's house, for example, that Egyptian priest's daughter whose beauty so impressed Setne-Khamwas in the famous Demotic story.[10] Like Aseneth, Tabubu lives in "a very lofty house," with "a wall around it," and "a garden on its north"—the type of tower-cum-courtyard structure that one sees in the beautiful Nilotic mosaic at Palestrina and in numerous Egyptian sites.[11] Even the spring ($\pi\eta\gamma\dot{\eta}$) in the courtyard is, as noted by Bonneau, exactly what we would expect in such an architectural complex.[12]

While this description of Aseneth's tower and courtyard certainly is based on our author's familiarity with the Egyptian countryside, we must also note that the detailed description of her garden clearly echoes Ezekiel's account of what he saw in his celebrated temple-vision (Ezek 40-8).[13] The spring which is "on the right" (cf. Ezek 47:1-2), the stream which flows from it (Ezek 47:2-6), the trees that grow there (Ezek 47:7) and their abundant fruit (Ezek 47:11-2), are all modeled after Ezekiel's description. This resemblance might seem insignificant, but it is the first hint that our author associates Aseneth's house with a temple.

4.2.2. The Tower and the Room

Having examined the court surrounding Aseneth's house, we turn to the "big and high" tower itself.

> And on top of that high tower there was an upper story with ten rooms. And the first room was big and beautiful—it was paved with

---

[10] Tr. M. Lichtheim, *Ancient Egyptian Literature*, 3:134-5.

[11] See P.G.P. Meyboom, *The Nile Mosaic*, 29-30, 40, and figs. 15-7, 27, 37, etc.; G. Husson, *OIKIA*, 45-54, 109-16, 147-51, 243-6, 248-51.

[12] D. Bonneau, "Les *realia* du paysage Égyptien," 213.

[13] See E.W. Smith, *Joseph and Asenath*, 63

purple stones, and its walls were faced with colored and precious stones, and its ceiling was made of gold. And inside that room, fastened to the walls, were the innumerable gods of the Egyptians, made of gold and silver (οἱ θεοὶ τῶν Ἀιγυπτίων ὧν οὐκ ἦν ἀριθμὸς χρυσοῖ καὶ ἀργυροῖ). And Aseneth worshipped them all and feared them and performed sacrifices to them every day (καὶ πάντας ἐκείνους ἐσέβετο Ἀσενὲθ καὶ ἐφοβεῖτο αὐτοὺς καὶ θυσίας αὐτοῖς ἐπετέλει καθ' ἡμέραν) (2:1-3).

A casual reading of this passage might make us think of an Egyptian maiden's beautifully adorned sleeping-room, not unlike that of Tabubu, who lives in the upper story of her tower, in a room which is "swept and adorned, its floor adorned with real lapis-lazuli and real turquoise," where the couches are "spread with royal linen," not unlike Aseneth's own bed (2:8).[14] These obvious similarities between Aseneth's room and Tabubu's provide further proof—if proof were needed—of the Egyptian coloring of *Joseph and Aseneth*, whose author knew quite well what an Egyptian priest's daughter's room might look like, and may even have been familiar with some of the conventions of the Egyptian novelistic tradition. Yet such similarities also serve to accentuate the difference between Aseneth's room and Tabubu's, namely, that inside the Helio-politan maiden's chamber, "fastened to the walls, were the innumerable gods of the Egyptians, made of gold and silver," and that "Aseneth worshipped them all and feared them and performed sacrifices to them every day." This description, perhaps influenced by Ezek 8:10, clearly sets Aseneth's room apart from Tabubu's, and, presumably, from that of all other Egyptian maidens. And lest someone doubt that it is within her own tower that Aseneth used to perform her sacrifices, we may note what happens later, when she gives up her idolatry:

And Aseneth hurried and took all her gods which were in her room, innumerable gods made of gold and silver, and ground them to shreds (συνέτριψεν αὐτοὺς εἰς λεπτά) and threw all the idols of the Egyptians (πάντα τὰ εἴδωλα τῶν Ἀιγυπτίων) through the window facing north from her upper story to the poor and needy. And Aseneth took her royal dinner—the fattlings, the fish, and the veal—and all the sacrifices of her gods (πάσας τὰς θυσίας τῶν θεῶν αὐτῆς) and the vessels of their wine of libation (τὰ σκεύη τοῦ οἴου τῆς σπουδῆς αὐτῶν) and threw everything through the window facing north, and gave everything to the strange dogs (10:12-3).

---

[14] Tr. Lichtheim, *ibid.*

It can hardly be a mere sleeping-room that houses not only all the gods but also "all their sacrifices" and "the vessels of their wine of libation." Aseneth, who used to "bless with her mouth dead and dumb idols and eat from their table bread of strangulation and drink from their libation a cup of treachery" (8:5), was conducting all these cultic activities within her private quarters. Adorned in her beautiful costume, with "the names of the gods of the Egyptians (τὰ ὀνόματα τῶν θεῶν τῶν Αἰγυπτίων) engraved everywhere on the bracelets and the stones, and the faces of all the idols (τὰ πρόσωπα τῶν εἰδώλων πάντων) carved on them" (3:6), she was performing daily sacrifices inside her secluded tower.

4.2.3. The κατ απέτ ασμα

If any doubt remains concerning the nature of Aseneth's tower, it is dispelled in light of the following passage, which opens the description of her repentance:

> And Aseneth rose from her bed and quietly went down the stairs from the upper story and went to the gate (εἰς τὸν πυλῶνα); and the doorkeeper (ἡ θυρουρός) was asleep with her children.[15] And Aseneth hurried and pulled down (καθεῖλεν) from the window the sheet of the curtain (τὴν δέρριν τοῦ καταπετάσματος),[16] and filled it with ashes from the hearth (τέφρας ἐκ τῆς ἑστίας),[17] and carried it up into the upper story, and put it on the floor (10:2).

The Greek word used here for "curtain," κατ απέτ ασμα, is such a rare word that we could base our entire argument on it alone. It is a word that appears almost exclusively in Jewish and Christian texts, and refers to the curtains which hung first in the Tabernacle, and then in the Jerusalem temple.[18] To a Jewish author, and to a Jewish audience, this word would have had an immediate cultic connotation. If Aseneth's

---

[15] For the *realia* behind the πυλῶν and the θυρουρός, cf. P.Mich. XI, 620.9.

[16] For δέρρις as "sheet" rather than "skin" cf. 10:14, and LXX Exod 26:7 etc., where δέρρις translates the Hebrew word יריעה.

[17] Or, perhaps, "from the altar," in which case this would have been the altar where Aseneth used to conduct her sacrifices. Unfortunately, ἑστία is a *hapax legomenon* in *Joseph and Aseneth*, but "hearth" seems the more likely meaning.

[18] C. Schneider, "κατ απέτ ασμα," 628-9. As far as I know, the tearing down of Aseneth's κατ απέτ ασμα has not been noted by New Testament scholars, in spite of its possible significance for the study of Mark 15:38 par.

tower is described as having a κατ απέτ ασμα, it must have been thought of, in some ways at least, as a temple.

4.2.4. "Graded Holiness"

To all the above considerations, one more may be added, namely, our author's notion of what scholars sometimes call "graded holiness." This first becomes apparent when Joseph enters Pentephres' court:

> And the gates of the court facing east were opened... and Joseph entered the court, and the gates of the court were closed, and every strange man or woman remained outside the court, because the guards of the gates drew tight and closed the doors, and all the strangers were shut out (5:4-6).

The two elements which emerge from this passage, the court's eastward orientation and the shutting out of all strangers, must have been of some importance to our author, since both are repeated elsewhere in the novel.[19] The first is, of course, quite understandable in a city called Heliopolis—"the City of the Sun"—and known to have been built on an east-west axis.[20] But the second element, the exclusion of all strangers (ἀλλότριοι), seems a bit unnecessary, and immediately brings to mind the exclusion of foreigners from the Jerusalem temple—and from Egyptian temples as well.[21]

It seems, however, that our author had a more elaborate scheme in mind. While the strangers are barred from entering the court, even more people are barred from Aseneth's tower, the inside of which no man has ever seen (2:1, 6; 7:7).[22] When it comes to Aseneth's room, only a select few are allowed entry—Aseneth, her virgins, and perhaps her mother, too (8:1). Finally, there is Aseneth's bed, on which no one else

---

[19] For the eastward orientation, not only of the court but of Aseneth's room too, see 2:7; 5:2; 11:1y, 15, 19; 14:1-3; 17:8. For the shutting out of strangers, see also 19:3.
[20] Apion, apud Josephus Ag.Ap. II.10 (M. Stern, Greek and Latin Authors, no. 164). For the archeological remains, see H. Ricke, "Eine Inventartafel," 128.
[21] For the Jerusalem temple, see Schürer (rev.), History, 2:285, and E.J. Bickerman, "The Warning Inscriptions," 389-94. For Egyptian temples see, e.g., Chaeremon, apud Porphyry, De Abstin. IV.6 (P.W. van der Horst, Chaeremon, 16-17, and n. 5).
[22] Note, however, the author's inconsistency here, since we later find two servant boys (18:1; 19:1), and Aseneth's male steward (18:2-5), entering her tower.

ever sat, only Aseneth herself (2:9; 15:14).[23] Thus, Aseneth's house has a central point—her bed—surrounded by three concentric circles: first her room, then her tower, then the court, outside of which lies the wider world. The further one goes toward the center, the less people are allowed entry.

We may, of course, interpret this element of our story merely as a literary device, meant to highlight the novel's romantic core—the hero's desire to penetrate the heroine's tower (and her bed)—but I doubt that this is what the author actually has in mind. In fact, it is the angel, and not Joseph, who eventually sits on Aseneth's bed (see below), and Joseph's entry into Aseneth's room goes unmentioned throughout the narrative (cf. 19:2). Thus, *Joseph and Aseneth*'s description of Aseneth's tower does not contribute to the romantic plot, and is unrelated to Joseph's relations with Aseneth. Rather, it seems that this description is yet another sign that Aseneth's tower is conceived of as a temple, with its strict rules of "graded holiness"—the further you enter the complex, the less people are allowed entry. This pattern is apparent in the biblical description of the desert tabernacle, in Ezekiel's temple-vision, in the detailed descriptions of the Jerusalem temple found in Josephus and in the Mishnah—and in many non-Jewish temples as well.[24]

Aseneth's tower, then, not only functions as a temple in which she sacrifices daily to all her gods, it also displays a temple-veil, and the entrance regulations which one would expect to find in such a structure. All this, however, applies only to the tower as it was in the beginning of the story, for within the narrative itself this structure undergoes a striking transformation, paralleling Aseneth's own conversion. It is this transformation, I would argue, that our author wishes to emphasize.

4.2.5. A House Converted

As noted above, one of Aseneth's first actions, once she repents of her idolatry (9:2), is to go downstairs and tear down the καταπέτασμα which hangs at the gate (10:2), that curtain which delimits a temple's sanctified

---

23 Did Aseneth, "adorned like a bride of (a) god (κεκοσμημένην ὡς νύμφην θεοῦ)" (4:1), expect her god to visit this untouched bed of hers? Cf., e.g., Herodotus II.182.
24 See P. Jenson, *Graded Holiness*, 37, 89-114, and J.Z. Smith, *To Take Place*, 47-73.

parts and separates the holy from the profane.[25] She next returns to her
room and grinds her idols to pieces, dispenses with their accessories,
and hurls everything out of her window, to be consumed by "the strange
dogs" (10:12-3). Thus, the main components of any "pagan" temple—the
idols and their sacrifices—are removed from Aseneth's room in this
second stage of the cleansing of her temple. She next strews ashes on
the floor of her chamber (10:14), and her bitter weeping, together with
the ashes, create "much mud" on the floor (10:16; cf. 11:17; 15:3), of
which she later says,

> Behold, the floor of my room, paved with colored and purple
> stones, which once was besprinkled with perfumes and wiped with
> bright cloths, is now besprinkled with my tears and was profaned
> (ἠτιμάσθη), being covered with ashes. Behold, my Lord, from my
> tears and the ashes much mud has been formed in my room, as on a
> broad street (13:6-7).

This, then, is the third stage of the desecration of Aseneth's temple—
after the tearing of the καταπέτασμα and the destruction of the idols
comes the profanation with ashes and tears.[26] The structure is now free
of any "pagan" remains, and ready to receive the "commander of the
house of the Most High" (14:8) and his divine message. With his arrival,
and especially once he agrees to sit on Aseneth's bed, which was "pure
and undefiled," for "no man or woman had ever sat on it" (15:4; cf. 2:9),
the structure's transformation from an idolatrous shrine to one fit for
the God of Israel has been approved. Together with Aseneth, her house
too has been converted.

How are we to explain this transformation, which seems to contribute nothing to *Joseph and Aseneth*'s plot? Apparently, the answer
must be sought not within the narrative, but in the author's sense of a
possible connection between two Heliopolitan landmarks of widely
different dates—Aseneth's tower-temple and Onias' temple-tower (cf.
above, Chapter 2.1.4).

That the two structures are not identical is easy to see: Aseneth's
court was surrounded by a stone wall with iron gates (2:10), Onias'

---

[25] One may compare here Iakimos' tearing down of one of the separating walls of
the Jerusalem temple's court, and the indignation provoked by this act—see 1
Macc 9:54-5; *Ant.* XII.413; m *Middot* 2:3, with Schürer (rev.), *History*, 1:175, n. 6).
Cf. also Mark 15:38 par.
[26] Is it the tears' salt which profanes the temple? For purification with salt, see,
e.g., Theocritus XXIV.97-8, with A.S.F. Gow, *Theocritus*, 2:431.

temple by a brick wall with stone gates (*War* VII.430). But they might still be intimately connected. After all, it is in Aseneth's room, on her lips and mouth, that the bee-priests build their new honeycomb-temple, once the angel urges them to leave their original home. And for Onias' followers, the claim that Aseneth's house had been located at exactly the same spot where they built their own temple would have been most welcome. If they indeed took a deserted pagan temple and built their new temple on it, as the letters quoted by Josephus claim (*Ant.* XIII.65-71)—and even if they merely were accused by their opponents of having done so—the assertion that this had once been Aseneth's house would have been doubly useful. First, it could serve as a counter-claim to Onias' Egyptian opponents, enraged at his appropriation of an ancient Egyptian temple.[27] If that Egyptian temple once belonged to Aseneth, then Onias was merely reclaiming property which—together with the "field of inheritance"—belonged to his distant ancestors. Second, such a claim could offset the charge made by Onias' Jewish opponents, and preserved in the forged letters quoted by Josephus, that Onias had built his temple in an inherently impure place, "full of sacred animals" (πλήρει ζῷων ἱερῶν, *Ant.* XIII.70). If it was Aseneth's deserted tower which lay beneath Onias' temple, the tower which she had desecrated, and whose purity was approved by the angel who appeared in her room and sat upon her bed, than the problem was far less acute.

To sum up: While *Joseph and Aseneth* provides no description of ancient Heliopolis, two specific sites within that city do receive special attention. One is the "field of inheritance," whose great productivity is stressed more than once—a field that belonged to Aseneth's parents, and then to Joseph and Aseneth themselves. The second is Aseneth's house, which is not only described at great length but also undergoes a transformation parallel to Aseneth's own conversion. Both elements have received scant scholarly attention in the past, and no attempt has ever been made to explain the significance of the large role they occupy in the narrative. Our own hypothesis, however, concerning the novel's origin, sheds new light on both Heliopolitan landmarks. For its Oniad readers, settled in and around Heliopolis, both Aseneth's "field of inheritance" and her house would have been of great importance, for each could supply—in its own way—a justification for the Jewish presence, and the Jewish temple, in Heliopolis.

---

[27] Note that CPJ III, 520 apparently mentions the Jews' desecration of the Egyptian temple(s)—Cf. G. Bohak, "CPJ III, 520," 33-4, and n. 4.

Chapter 5

The Oniad Eschatology of *Joseph and Aseneth*

While reading the honeycomb scene, in Chapter 1, we noted that the angel's promises to Aseneth may be divided into two types—those which are fulfilled within the narrative framework of *Joseph and Aseneth*, and those which are not. Among the first type may be included his promises (a) that she would be renewed and fashioned anew, etc. (15:5; cf. 8:9) and that her flesh would bloom like flowers of life, etc. (16:16), which are fulfilled when she acquires such supernatural beauty that even Joseph cannot recognize her (18:9-11; 19:4; cf. 20:6; 21:4); (b) that she would eat blessed bread of life, etc. (15:5), which, as the angel insists, is fulfilled in 16:16; (c) that Joseph would come to her (15:10), fulfilled in chapter 18; and (d) that she would be his bride (15:6), fulfilled in chapter 21.

All these promises are fulfilled—but what about those that are not? Naturally, the interpretation of the honeycomb scene as containing a symbolic depiction of the events of the distant future presents a new vantage point from which to examine this aspect of the angel's visit, for it now seems likely that these promises were meant to be fulfilled not within Aseneth's lifetime, but at the time when the bee-priests would leave their honeycomb-temple and establish a new one in Heliopolis.

Pursuing such a line of inquiry, we will focus on the eschatology of *Joseph and Aseneth*, that is, on those events which its author and early readers had seen with their own eyes, or were expecting to see in the near future. For it was they, and not Aseneth, who were the real beneficiaries of most of the promises made to her so many years earlier.

5.1. A "City of Refuge"

The most obvious aspect of the eschatology of *Joseph and Aseneth* is the recurrent use, in the descriptions of Aseneth's future status, of terms and motifs borrowed from biblical passages concerning the future Jerusalem. This is evident when the angel first promises Aseneth that her name shall no longer be Aseneth, but "City of Refuge (πόλις καταφυγῆς),"

> because in you many nations will find refuge with the Lord, the Most High God (ἐν σοὶ καταφεύξονται ἔθνη πολλὰ ἐπὶ κύριον τὸν θεὸν τὸν ὕψιστον), and under your wings will be sheltered many peoples who trust in the Lord God (καὶ ὑπὸ τὰς πτέρυγάς σου σκεπασθήσονται λαοὶ πολλοὶ πεποιθότες ἐπὶ κυρίῳ τῷ θεῷ), and within your walls will be guarded those who attach themselves to the Most High God in the name of Repentance (καὶ ἐν τῷ τείχει σου διαφυλαχθήσονται οἱ προσκείμενοι τῷ θεῷ τῷ ὑψίστῳ ἐν ὀνόματι τῆς μετανοίας) (15:7).

As noted by Burchard, this passage displays a close verbal resemblance to Zechariah's promise to Jerusalem that "many nations will take refuge with the Lord (καταφεύξονται ἔθνη πολλὰ ἐπὶ τὸν κύριον)" and will dwell in its midst "on that day" (LXX Zech 2:15).[1] When speaking of Aseneth's future status, *Joseph and Aseneth* employs one of the commonest eschatological motifs in the Hebrew Bible, its Greek translation, and subsequent Jewish literature, that of the conversion of the Gentiles. Aseneth, herself a repentant Egyptian maiden, is destined to become a city into which future converts would flee, a role normally reserved for the eschatological Jerusalem herself.

The woman-as-city imagery reappears a few verses later, when the angel promises Aseneth that she shall be "like a walled mother-city (ὡς μητρόπολις τετειχισμένη) of all those who seek refuge in the name of the Lord God, the king of the ages (πάντων τῶν καταφευγόντων ἐπὶ τῷ ὀνόματι κυρίου τοῦ θεοῦ τοῦ βασιλέως τῶν αἰώνων)" (16:6). Here too the terms used are commonly associated with Jerusalem, for ancient Jews were supposed to have only one mother-city. It was Jerusalem, which "because of its temple"—says Josephus—was "the mother-city of the whole Jewish nation."[2] But who does the author have in mind here,

---

[1] Ch. Burchard, *Untersuchungen*, 119; cf. LXX Isa 54:15: προσήλυτοι... ἐπὶ σὲ καταφεύξονται.
[2] Josephus, *War* VII.375 (ἡ τοῦ παντὸς Ἰουδαίων γένους μητρόπολις), *Ant.* III.245 (εἰς ἐκείνην τὴν πόλιν, ἣν διὰ τὸν ναὸν μητρόπολιν ἕξουσιν); cf. *Ant.* XI.160; *War* II.400

when speaking of "all those who seek refuge in the name of the Lord God"? Is he thinking of proselytes only, or of born Jews as well? After all, the language here is reminiscent not only of LXX Zech 2:15 but of LXX Jer 27(50):5 as well—a verse which speaks of Jews, not proselytes, who "will take refuge with the Lord God (καταφεύξονται πρὸς κύριον τὸν θεόν)" in Zion.

The future refugees' identity is further clarified in a subsequent passage, when the angel tells Aseneth's seven virgins that they shall be the "seven pillars of the City of Refuge," and that "all those (fem.) who join the chosen ones of that city (αἱ σύνοικοι τῶν ἐκλεκτῶν τῆς πόλεως ἐκείνης)" will rest upon them forever (17:6). As noted in Chapter 1.5, the reference to the seven pillars echoes Prov 9:1—"Wisdom has built her house, she has hewn her seven pillars"—and hints at Aseneth's future role as a place of great wisdom, yet another image which may have been influenced by Jerusalem-centered language.[3] The dwellers of Aseneth's city, moreover, are here referred to as "the chosen ones" and all those who join them. Finally, Joseph's words to Aseneth are even clearer:

> The Lord God founded your walls in the highest, and your walls are adamantine walls of life, for the sons of the living God (οἱ υἱοὶ τοῦ ζῶντος θεοῦ) will dwell in your City of Refuge, and the Lord God will be their king forever (19:8).

In light of such passages, there is no doubt that not only "many nations" will dwell in Aseneth's "City of Refuge," but also "the chosen ones" and "the sons of God." As noted in Chapter 1.3-5, *Joseph and Aseneth* applies these terms not only to proselytes but to born Jews as well, such as Joseph, the priestly bees, and the people whom God "has chosen before all things came into being" (8:9). It seems, in fact, that as in other Jewish and Early Christian texts, "the chosen ones (of God)" are those who remain steadfast in their worship of the Lord in spite of many trials and tribulations, and in return are promised great rewards with the coming of the *eschaton*.[4] Moreover, once we realize that it is not only

---

etc.; LXX Isa 1:26 (!); Philo, *Flacc* 46; *Leg. ad Gaium*, 203, 281, 295 etc., and A. Kasher, "Jerusalem as a 'Metropolis'."

[3] See esp. *Sira* 24:1-12 and J.C.H. Lebram, "Jerusalem, Wohnsitz der Weisheit," 114, 119-20. For a similar use of Prov 9:1, cf. *Herm. Vis.* III.8.1-8.

[4] See, e.g.,*1 Enoch* 1; 5:7-10; 25:5-6; 1QH 2.13; 14.15; 1QS 8.6; 1QpHab 5.4; 10.13; Mk. 13:14-27; Mt. 24:20-31 etc.

proselytes, but born Jews as well who would one day join Aseneth's "City of Refuge," it becomes quite likely that even "those who attach themselves to the Most High God in the name of Repentance (οἱ προσκείμενοι τῷ θεῷ τῷ ὑψίστῳ ἐν ὀνόματι τῆς μετανοίας)" in 15:7 are not only Gentiles who repent of their idolatry, but repentant Jews as well.[5] These would be persons such as Dan, Gad, Naphthali, and Asher, who are spared by their brothers (28:2-17), or the wicked bee-priests, who are given a second chance once their wicked plot fails (16:23). Such persons, if and when they repent of their sins, probably may join "the chosen ones" and "the sons of God," and live in the "City of Refuge."

The author's description of Aseneth, then, is not that of "das Zion der Proselyten," as suggested by Burchard, nor is she "das himmlische Jerusalem," to use Fischer's words, in spite of her walls being "founded upon a rock of the seventh heaven" (22:13).[6] Rather, she is destined to become an eschatological Jerusalem, which will be established at some distant time and in which Jews and proselytes will live together, forever.

This description of Aseneth's future is intimately connected with the symbolic vision revealed to her. As noted in Chapter 1.4, the priestly-bees, goaded by the angel's incisions in their honeycomb and by his explicit command ("Come," 16:17y), leave their honeycomb-temple and establish a new one, similar to the first, on Aseneth's lips and mouth. In this manner, the angel reveals to Aseneth that one day a group of Jewish priests would leave the Jerusalem temple and build a new one, similar to the one they left behind, within her city—and perhaps even in her very room (cf. above, Chapter 4.2.5). This revelation sheds further light on the description of Aseneth herself as a would-be Jerusalem, and helps elucidate the angel's promises concerning her future inhabitants. Both the vision and the promises, which go unfulfilled throughout the narrative, refer to the arrival in Heliopolis of the Jewish priests from Jerusalem, and the subsequent establishment of their own temple, their New Jerusalem.

As noted in Chapter 2.1.4, Onias' temple was modeled after the one in Jerusalem, and its supporters described it as the true "City of Righteousness" of which Isaiah had spoken. Thus, the use of Jerusalem-related idioms in *Joseph and Aseneth*'s description of its heroine is hardly surprising. Nor is it a mere coincidence that the description of

---

[5] The verb προσκεῖμαι, at least, is not used to describe proselytes only, for Levi too is said to be προσκείμενος πρὸς τὸν κύριον (22:13)—cf. above, Chapter 3.3.

[6] Ch. Burchard, *Untersuchungen*, 119; U. Fischer, *Eschatologie*, 115.

Aseneth's "field of inheritance" echoes biblical passages relating to Paradise and to the Promised Land (cf. Chapter 4.1), and that Aseneth's courtyard is described in terms borrowed from Ezekiel's temple-vision (cf. Chapter 4.2.1). For *Joseph and Aseneth*'s Oniad readers, Aseneth's transformation into a "City of Refuge" and a New Jerusalem was an angelic promise come true, fulfilled in their own day by their own (divinely sanctioned) actions. Moreover, their Jerusalem-on-the-Nile was a "City of Refuge" not only for "the sons of the living God," but also for "many nations," in line with Isaiah's prophecy:[7]

> In that day there shall be five cities in Egypt speaking the language of Canaan and swearing by the name of the Lord; one of them shall be called the City of Asedek (πόλις ασεδεκ).[8] In that day there shall be an altar (θυσιαστήριον) to the Lord in the land of Egypt, and a pillar (στήλη) for the Lord upon her frontier. And it shall stand forever (εἰς τὸν αἰῶνα) as a sign for the Lord[9] in the land of Egypt; for they will cry to him because of their oppressors, and the Lord will send them a man who will save them, judging and saving them. And the Lord shall be known to the Egyptians; and the Egyptians shall know the Lord on that day, and they shall make sacrifices (ποιήσουσιν θυσίας) and make vows to the Lord and pay them (εὔξονται εὐχὰς τῷ κυρίῳ καὶ ἀποδώσουσιν). And the Lord shall strike the Egyptians a heavy blow, and heal them with a healing; and they shall turn to the Lord, and he shall hear them and heal them (LXX Isa 19:18-22).

To its Oniad readers, believing that Isaiah's prophecy was being fulfilled (cf. above, Chapter 2.1.2), the clear implication of this passage was that their temple must serve not only its Jewish founders (led by "a man who will save them"?),[10] but also the many Egyptians who will come to worship the Lord and sacrifice on His behalf.[11]

Unfortunately, we have no way of judging how many non-Jews, if any, actually joined the Oniad community. The only available sources— the tombstones excavated in Tell-el-Yahoudieh and Demerdash, or

---

[7] I translate the LXX text, noting the most significant divergences from the MT.

[8] I.e., "City of Righteousness." 1QIsᵃ reads "City of the Sun" here, and MT "City of Destruction." Cf. below, Chapter 6.4.

[9] MT: "it shall stand as a sign and a reminder for the Lord" (the Greek translator read כָּעֵד instead of וּלְעֵד).

[10] Whether these expectations are connected with the mysterious "King from the Sun" (*Sib. Or.* III.652) or "the King from the City of the Sun" (*Apoc. El.* 2:46), are questions that I hope to explore elsewhere.

[11] For another possible example of a connection made between the events of the 160s BCE and the conversion of the Gentiles, see *Sib. Or.* III.601-34; but cf. Schürer (rev.), *History*, 3:637.

purchased in neighboring villages—display some Egyptian names,[12] but these need not necessarily have been Egyptian converts. Rather, they are more likely to have been Jews who bore Egyptian names, or even "ordinary" Egyptians who had nothing to do with Onias' temple and happened to be buried in the Land of Onias before, after, or even during the Jewish presence there.[13] But the Egyptians' willingness to join the temple need not have been commensurate with the Oniad desire for them to do so. Aseneth became the "City of Refuge" for all those who would follow in her footsteps, as it were, on the path "from death to life" (8:9), but her generous offer may have found very few takers.

5.2. A "Place of Rest" in Heaven

In addition to the earthly "City of Refuge," our author also envisages a heavenly "place of rest" for all "the chosen ones," and those who join them. This location is first mentioned by Joseph, in his short prayer to God upon meeting Aseneth:

> ...and count her among your people, whom you have chosen before all things came into being; and let her enter your rest, which you have prepared for your chosen ones (εἰς τὴν κατάπαυσίν σου ἣν ἡτοίμασας τοῖς ἐκλεκτοῖς σου), and live in your eternal life forever (ζησάτω ἐν τῇ αἰωνίῳ ζωῇ σου εἰς τὸν αἰῶνα χρόνον) (8:9).

From a subsequent passage, we learn that it was not God himself, but his daughter, Repentance, who "prepared a place of rest in heaven for all those who repent (πᾶσι τοῖς μετανοοῦσι τόπον ἀναπαύσεως ἡτοίμασεν ἐν τοῖς οὐρανοῖς)," and that "she will renew all those who repent, and she will serve them forever" (15:7). It is, presumably, this uranological site that Levi, the far-sighted prophet, had access to, for he "loved Aseneth very much, and saw her place of rest in the highest (καὶ ἑώρα τὸν τόπον τῆς καταπαύσεως αὐτῆς ἐν τοῖς ὑψίστοις)" (22:13).

Like Aseneth's "City of Refuge," this "place of rest," and the entire heavenly realm, have been prepared for a variety of potential residents. Heaven, of course, is where the angel comes from (14:2-3; 19:5), and it is "to heaven, to his place (εἰς τὸν οὐρανὸν εἰς τὸν τόπον αὐτοῦ)" that he

---

[12] E.g., Phabeis, JIGRE 33 (CIJ 1510); Phameis, JIGRE 34 (CIJ 1511); Paos, JIGRE 114 (CIJ 1489), etc.
[13] Cf. G. Bohak, "Good Jews, Bad Jews."

returns once his visit is over. The good bees, too, when ordered to "go to their place," immediately go there (16:20-1). The bad bees, on the other hand, are sent to Aseneth's courtyard—apparently, they must repent of their behavior before they too will be allowed into heaven. Moreover, since the honeycomb "is a comb of life, and whoever eats from it will not die forever" (16:14), it seems clear that many are destined to share the bliss of Aseneth's eternal life and unending youth (15:4; 16:16; cf. 8:9; 27:10). Indeed, all those who take part in the Jerusalem temple cult, and who subsequently take part in that of Onias' temple—as the good bees do in 16:20—will certainly join her. They will be registered in "the book of the living,"[14] right after her name (cf. 15:4), and so, secluded and sheltered, they shall live happily ever after in that heavenly "place of rest" prepared by God and his lovely daughter, Repentance.

5.3. The Burning Honeycomb

As noted in Chapter 1.5, the honeycomb scene ends after the angel burns the original honeycomb while ignoring the second comb, the one on Aseneth's mouth. This action probably should be read as a part of the symbolic revelation itself, for any other interpretation would leave open the question of why only one honeycomb was burnt, while the other was left intact. To this argument another may now be added, based on the parallels between the honeycomb scene and the brotherly feud of chapters 22-9. For when Dan, Gad, Naphthali, and Asher lie in ambush, the latter two express their fear that God is on Joseph's side "and he will send fire from heaven and it will consume (καταφάγεται) us, and God's angels will fight against us on his behalf" (25:6). This clearly echoes 17:3, where the angel causes a fire to come forth, a fire which "consumed (κατέφαγε) the comb."[15] If the honeycomb stands for the Jerusalem temple, the angel's destruction thereof resembles what Naphthali and Asher were afraid of, namely, God's fiery destruction of those who oppose Joseph, Aseneth, and her eschatological "City of Refuge."

Even this parallel, however, does not yet explain what the burning honeycomb would have meant to *Joseph and Aseneth*'s author, for the

---

[14] For which cf. Dan. 12:1; *Jub.* 30:22; *1 Enoch* 108:3 etc.
[15] These are the only appearances of καταφαγεῖν (or κατεσθίω) in the novel. Cf. Aseneth's statement that the bad brothers' swords had "melted like wax before fire (ὥσπερ κηρὸς ἀπὸ προσώπου πυρός)" (28:10), perhaps another echo of 17:3.

symbolic reference to the future destruction of the Jerusalem temple could have originated in two very different historical contexts. On the one hand, it could have been written after the Jerusalem temple indeed was burnt, and Onias' temple remained, for some four years, the only Jewish temple. In such a case, this section of *Joseph and Aseneth* must be dated to some time between 70 and 74 CE, and is yet another *vaticinium ex eventu*. Yet given the recurrent impression (Chapter 3.1-2) that the novel as a whole would fit a Ptolemaic context better than a Roman one, we probably would be forced to postulate an early-70s CE interpolation into an older version of our novel. This is, to be sure, not impossible, but another possibility seems much more likely, namely, that the symbolic reference to the burning of the Jerusalem temple is not a description of a past event, but the author's expectation of the future. As in other such scenes, the angel reveals to Aseneth not only the events leading up to the author's own time, but also events that the author was hoping to see. Enoch's visions, for example, "foretold" not only the persecution of 167 BCE, which the author of the *Animal Apocalypse* (*1 Enoch* 85-90) must have witnessed, but also the Judgment (90:20-39), which never came to pass. Similarly, *Joseph and Aseneth*'s Oniad author included in his revelation scene not only the establishment of Onias' temple, but also the miraculous destruction of the rival temple in Jerusalem, leaving Aseneth's "City of Refuge" as the one and only Jerusalem in the coming *eschaton*. Once this promise too would be fulfilled, it will be in Heliopolis, and only there, that "the sons of the living God will dwell... and the Lord God will reign as king over them forever" (19:8). We know, but he could not have known, that his wish was eventually fulfilled, and that the Jerusalem temple indeed was destroyed. We also know, however, that his own "City of Refuge" was quick to follow.

Chapter 6

Rereading *Joseph and Aseneth*

We have spent quite some time analyzing specific scenes of *Joseph and Aseneth*, and delving into some of its smaller details. It is now time to put the magnifying lens aside and look at the larger picture. It is time, that is, to ask some questions about the novel as a whole: who wrote it, when, and for whom? What was the author's purpose in writing his novel, and why did he write it in such a way? Finally, we shall briefly examine the novel's subsequent history, when it found readers whom its author never had in mind.

6.1. Author

As noted in the previous chapters, there are several things we can now say about *Joseph and Aseneth*'s author, beyond the broad scholarly consensus outlined in the introduction. First, he seems to have been intimately connected with Onias' temple, insisting that Onias' actions were foretold to Aseneth by the supreme commander of God's divine host, and supplying further "evidence" that could serve to justify Onias' move. Second, in addition to his good knowledge of Greek, at least in its "Septuagintal" variety, and in spite of his general dislike of Egyptians, he shows some familiarity with Egyptian (Heliopolitan) theology, and perhaps even with the Egyptian novelistic tradition. Third, his thought-world is deeply imbued with eschatological expectations, believing as he does that Aseneth's "City of Refuge" will shelter "the sons of God" and "many nations," and that "the Lord God will be their king forever."

Naturally, one would wish to know more about *Joseph and Aseneth*'s author, but he clearly preferred to hide his own identity behind the biblicizing narrative. In fact, it is quite likely that the best portrait of our author we will ever have is the one he himself has left us, when speaking of his distant ancestor:

> Levi... was attached to the Lord (ἦν προσκείμενος πρὸς τὸν κύριον), and he was a wise man (ἀνὴρ συνίων) and a prophet of the Most High (προφήτης ὑψίστου) and sharp-sighted with his eyes, and he saw letters written in heaven by the finger of God and he knew the unspeakable (mysteries) of the Most High God and secretly revealed them to Aseneth (καὶ ᾔδει τὰ ἄρρητα θεοῦ τοῦ ὑψίστου καὶ ἀπεκάλυπτεν αὐτὰ τῇ Ἀσενὲθ κρυφῇ), for Levi loved Aseneth very much, and he saw her place of rest in the highest, and her walls like adamantine eternal walls, and her foundations founded upon a rock of the seventh heaven (22:11-3).

It is in his description of Levi, I would argue, that the author's own identity comes closest to the narrative surface. He is—in his own eyes, at least—a prophet and a visionary, well aware of God's unspeakable mysteries and secret plans. He is a brave and pious soldier, always forgiving a vanquished foe and never harming a wayward brother. And he is, most of all, deeply loyal to Aseneth and to her "City of Refuge"— that "City of Righteousness" where he actually lived. Eating "blessed bread of life," drinking "a blessed cup of immortality," and anointing himself with "a blessed ointment of incorruptibility," this Heliopolitan priest counted himself among "the sons of God" and "the chosen ones of God" who were chosen "before all things came into being." Naturally, he was also hoping to go to that heavenly "place of rest" prepared for them all—that wonderful site that his forefather, Levi, used to see.

6.2. Date

Dating our author is a more difficult task, since he carefully avoids any obvious anachronisms in his biblicizing novel. He never explicitly refers to the Greek (or Roman) presence in Egypt, and does his best to use biblical and/or archaizing terminology—note such terms as ἄρχων (1:3 etc.), σατράπης (1:3 etc.), or ἑταῖροι (23:3)—so as not to disclose his own time of writing. Even in the few cases where he does borrow a contemporary *terminus technicus*—such as his use of κλῆρος to describe Pentephres' field (10:1), or of φίλοι as a court-title (23:4)—these terms are too common in the ancient world to warrant any specific dating.[1]

In spite of these difficulties, I believe that a good case can be made for dating the book to the mid-second century, sometime between 160 and 145 BCE, for the following reasons:

1) General atmosphere: As noted in Chapter 3.1-2, both the favorable attitude toward Pharaoh and the great emphasis on the Patriarchs' military prowess would suggest a Ptolemaic, not Roman, date for *Joseph and Aseneth*. Moreover, our author stresses the close links between the Jews and Pharaoh, which might reflect the relations between his own community and "Pharaoh"—the Ptolemaic ruler in whose army he probably served. The obvious candidate in such a case would be Ptolemy VI Philometor (180-145 BCE), Onias' generous benefactor, a king whose reign saw Egypt's Jews prosperous, self-confident, and secure in their expectations of a glorious future.[2] It is in this period, more than any other, that *Joseph and Aseneth*'s optimism, assertiveness, and pride would find their most suitable historical context.

2) The burning honeycomb: If the author indeed was hoping for the destruction of the Jerusalem temple (cf. Chapter 5.3), he must have lived in the very early days of Onias' temple's existence. As noted above (Chapter 2.2.2), in 103 BCE Ananias was presented with a golden opportunity to attack Jerusalem and regain the high priesthood, or destroy its temple—and declined. This decision apparently marked the final truce between the Oniads and the victorious Hasmonean dynasty. *Joseph and Aseneth*, with its wish for the miraculous destruction of the Jerusalem temple, probably belongs in an earlier period. In fact, it might even be argued that Ananias' refusal to attack Jerusalem was partly motivated by his own familiarity with *Joseph and Aseneth*, and his belief that a divine fire, and not a human conflagration, would consume the Jerusalem temple. A pious man, Ananias may have known, must never repay evil for evil, nor attack his Jewish brothers with a sword.

---

[1] For κλῆρος, see Cl. Préaux, *L'Économie royale*, 463-80; for φίλοι, see above, Chapter 4, n. 7.
[2] See V. Tcherikover, CPJ 1:19-21, and the historical survey above, Chapter 2.

3) Aseneth as a "City of Refuge:" As noted in Chapter 5.1, the description of Aseneth as a future "City of Refuge" for "many nations," for "many peoples who trust in the Lord God," for "those who attach themselves to the Most High God in the name of Repentance," and for "the sons of the living God," is deeply influenced by biblical passages relating to the status of the eschatological Jerusalem. Moreover, this description probably reflects the eschatological fervor which led Onias and his followers to believe that Isaiah's ancient prophecy (Isa 19:18-25) was being fulfilled in their own day.

Our knowledge of Oniad history is quite sketchy, yet one thing is clear. Whatever hope the Oniads had that in their own day "the Lord shall be known to the Egyptians, and the Egyptians shall know the Lord" (Isa 19:21), this hope did not materialize. As noted in Chapter 2.2-3, their temple's heyday was in the second century BCE—the next two centuries were characterized by protracted decline, and finally utter destruction. Whatever eschatological expectations the Oniad Jews entertained, they probably did not last for long. *Joseph and Aseneth*, with its emphasis on Aseneth's "City of Refuge," and on the "many nations" destined to join it, probably belongs in the earlier days of the Oniad presence in Egypt.

4) Ioakim: In Chapter 3.7, we noted that the only non-biblical figure in *Joseph and Aseneth* to receive a personal name is the king of Moab, Ioakim. Thus, the possibility suggested itself that the author inserted into his story the name of Onias' rival to the Jerusalem high priesthood. If this indeed is the case, then *Joseph and Aseneth* probably was written not many years after Iakimos' high priesthood (162-159 BCE), for it is hard to imagine a later author still intrigued by an ancient rival's name. For this to happen, the memory of Iakimos' usurpation of the Jerusalem high priesthood must have been quite fresh.

All these arguments cannot be said to constitute an unambiguous demonstration that *Joseph and Aseneth* was written in the mid-second century BCE, and later dates cannot be ruled out. It should be stressed, however, that the main argument commonly adduced against such an early date—that the author was already familiar with much of the Greek Bible—is extremely tenuous.[3] As Sirah's grandson informs us, by 132 BCE the Pentateuch, the Prophets, and other ancient texts were

---

[3] E.g., A.-M. Denis, *Introduction*, 47; Ch. Burchard, *Untersuchungen*, 144.

available in their Greek translations.[4] Moreover, other Jewish writers
of the 150s BCE, such as Eupolemus, clearly demonstrate a familiarity
with the Greek Bible even beyond the Pentateuch.[5] There is, therefore,
no basis to the claim that a mid-second century author could not have
been familiar with quite a few biblical books in their Greek versions.[6]

6.3. Intended Readers

The discussion of *Joseph and Aseneth*'s author immediately raises a
closely related question: who was meant to read this novel? The text
itself never refers to its intended readers, but its style, and some of the
narrative details, furnish important clues. First, *Joseph and Aseneth* is
written in a heavily biblicized idiom, which would have made it quite
appalling to any well educated Greek. Phrases such as "my face had
fallen," "cut them down in the mouth of the sword," "by death shall he
die," and countless others would have seemed bizarre, not to say unin-
telligible, to anyone not familiar with the Jewish Bible.[7] Other features,
such as the undeclined personal names,[8] or the constant parataxis (καί...
καί... καί) would have irritated even the most undiscerning of readers.[9]
Second, our author takes it for granted that his readers are already
familiar with Joseph, Jacob, Levi, and their previous exploits, from
Joseph's foreknowledge of the coming famine (4:7), to Simeon and Levi's
slaughter of the Shechemites (23:2, 14). Anyone who was not familiar
with the book of Genesis would have found *Joseph and Aseneth* very
hard to follow.[10]

---

[4] See LXX Sir, Prologue, and Schürer (rev.), *History*, 3:476-7.
[5] See, e.g., C.R. Holladay, *Fragments*, 1:95, 100-1, n. 14. For Eupolemus' writings,
see further below, Chapter 6.5.
[6] Ch. Burchard, *Untersuchungen*, 148-51, adduces lexical evidence for dating
Joseph and Aseneth not earlier than 100 BCE, but, as he himself admits, the state
of Hellenistic lexicography, and of Judeo-Greek literature, precludes any reliance
on such methods for securely dating our text.
[7] τὸ πρόσωπόν μου συμπέπτωκε (13:9; 18:3-4, 7); κατέκοψαν αὐτοὺς ἐν στόματι
ῥομφαίας (26:5); θανάτῳ ἀποθανεῖται (21:8).
[8] Cf. Josephus' remark in *Ant.* I.129.
[9] It certainly had this effect on some later readers, whose efforts to improve
Joseph and Aseneth's Greek are visible in recensions *a* and *c* of the novel (cf.
Appendix 1, below).
[10] See G. Delling, "Einwirkungen," and R.D. Chesnutt, *From Death to Life*, 256-8.

Writing in a biblicizing idiom and assuming his readers' familiarity with ancient Jewish narratives, our author was virtually giving up on the possibility of reaching a wide non-Jewish audience. Yet by choosing the Jews' hallowed ancestors for his protagonists, and by giving his narrative such a distinct biblical flavor, he was endowing it with greater authority for his Jewish readers. Any claim that he wished to make by writing this novel would have benefited from the aura of age and sanctity that its biblical style would have had in the eyes and mind of any Jewish reader.

We might, however, wish to be even more specific, for it seems likely that its intended readers were first and foremost the Oniad Jews themselves. While most contemporary Jewish readers probably would have noted the honeycomb scene's apocalyptic tone, and the priestly aspect of the bees' outward appearance, it is far from certain that they would have grasped the novel's meaning in its entirety. Moreover, nowhere in *Joseph and Aseneth* does the author address the needs and concerns of readers who are not among "the chosen ones of God," nor does he try to convince them to follow his lead and settle in Heliopolis. Our novel, it seems, was meant to be read mainly by those who already were convinced.

6.4. Purpose

Having discussed *Joseph and Aseneth*'s author and intended readers, we must now ask what it was that this author was trying to say. In a way, this is the most important question for the present study, since it is here that our interpretation of the novel differs most radically from previous scholars' views.

It is not uncommon for modern readers of *Joseph and Aseneth* to assume that it first came into being when some ancient Jewish readers of Gen 41:45 were troubled by Joseph's marriage to an Egyptian girl, the daughter of a pagan priest. The novel, according to this view, is one reader's attempt to explain how this seemingly unbecoming union came about. By stressing that the marriage followed Aseneth's conversion from an idol-worshiper to a devout follower of the God of Israel, the embarrassed author removed that apparent difficulty. While doing so, he also turned her conversion into a model for future generations of converts, and especially those of his own day.[11]

This common view of the novel's origins and meaning is, in my view, far from satisfactory. First, we must stress that only a small part of the novel is devoted to Aseneth's metamorphosis from a worshiper of the Egyptian gods to a pious Jewess, and her conversion itself is described in just one short sentence—"and she cried a great and bitter cry, and repented of all the gods whom she had worshipped, and spurned all her idols" (9:2). Second, her repentance is motivated not by a noble religious conviction, but by Joseph's beauty, and his blatant refusal to marry an idolatrous woman. This is not the best paradigm for the future conversion of "many nations." Third, the fact that it is Pharaoh who conducts the elaborate wedding ceremony, and that both the king and Pentephres are repeatedly described as acknowledging the Jewish God and admiring the Jewish faith (e.g., 3:3-4; 4:7; 18:11; 20:7; 21:4-6), indicates that the author did not envisage as great a gap separating Jews from Gentiles as his modern interpreters suggest.[12] Fourth, in spite of some Egyptians' willingness to acknowledge God, and contrary to what we might have expected, Aseneth's move does not trigger any other conversions. Even her virgin maidens, the "seven pillars of (her) City of Refuge" (18:6), are not said to have renounced their idolatry and turned to the true God of Israel. Fifth, the dichotomy between good and bad brothers, a dichotomy that preceded Aseneth's conversion and was unaffected by it, seems rather out of place in a text which sets out to create an ideal paradigm for the author's own day. Sixth, Aseneth's conversion is not accompanied by any study of the precepts of her new faith, nor does she observe any Jewish practices after her conversion. For a novel that focuses on the issue of conversion, such an omission would be quite puzzling. Seventh, much of the novel, and especially the honeycomb scene, remains enigmatic and inexplicable within this framework. Finally, the transfer to a Heliopolitan maiden of images and phrases normally reserved for the eschatological Jerusalem makes little sense within this interpretative model, for why would anyone not

---

[11] For diverse formulations of this view see, e.g., V. Aptowitzer, "Asenath," 239; M. Philonenko, *Joseph et Aséneth*, 53-61; A. Momigliano, *Alien Wisdom*, 117-8; Ch. Burchard, "Joseph and Aseneth," 177, 189; J.J. Collins, *Between Athens and Jerusalem*, 211; J. Mélèze Modrzejewski, *Les juifs d'Égypte*, 60-4.

[12] Note also 20:8, where Jews and Egyptians suddenly eat together, in spite of 7:1.

use the real Jerusalem for this purpose, unless his relations with that city were at the very root of the problem?

Given these difficulties, it seems to me that this standard model may safely be replaced by a completely different reconstruction of how and why *Joseph and Aseneth* came into being. The origins of our novel must be sought neither in an embarrassed reader's reaction to Gen 41:45 nor in his desire to write a seductive missionary pamphlet. Instead, its origins should be traced to Onias' arrival in Heliopolis, the construction of his temple there, and the various reactions to this move. Many Jews objected to the establishment of a Jewish temple away from Jerusalem, and insisted—as both Josephus and Philo would, vehemently—that Jews should have only one temple.[13] Some of Onias' opponents even claimed that this temple was built in an inherently impure place, "full of sacred animals" (*Ant.* XIII.70), and, in Tcherikover's words, "quite unsuited for the needs of the worship of the God of Israel."[14] Many Egyptians, on the other hand, objected to the Jews' settlement in and around Heliopolis, a venerated Egyptian cultural center, to the allotment of this region as a Jewish κατοικία, and perhaps even to their use of a deserted Egyptian shrine for the erection of their own temple.[15] This Egyptian hatred would remain evident even in the first century CE, with Apion's attack on Onias and Dositheus. His calumnies, as Josephus reports, included a vicious pun on Onias' name—no doubt deriving 'Ονίας from ὄνος, "ass," the emblem of the Seth, leader of all intrusive foreigners.[16]

In light of such objections, it was natural for the Heliopolitan Jews to look for ways in which to justify their actions. One way of doing so was to quote Isa 19:18-9, the ancient prophecy that foretold how one day there would be an altar to God in Egypt, in "the City of the Sun." Onias' followers—whose arrival in Heliopolis was motivated by this prophetic

---

[13] See Deut 12:4-7, 11-4, 17-8; and Philo, *Spec. Leg.* I.67; Josephus, *Ant.* IV.200-1; XII.54 (cf. 1 Macc 10:38); *Ag.Ap.* II.193

[14] V. Tcherikover, *Hellenistic Civilization*, 278.

[15] See G. Bohak, "CPJ III, 520," with *Sib. Or.* V.68 (quoted above, Chapter 3.5); cf. J. Yoyotte, "L'Égypte ancienne," 134; A. Zivie, "Tell el Yahoudieh," 15-6; C. Aziza, "L'utilization polémique," 56-7.

[16] *Apud* Josephus, *Ag.Ap.* II.49-56 (note II.50, clearly meant to give Onias' action an anti-Roman character that it never had). For Apion's pun, cf. Thackeray's note in LCL *Josephus*, 1:312, and the similar pun on the Persian king Artaxerxes Ochus (᾽Ωχος-ὄνος) in Plutarch, *De Iside*, 31 (*Mor.* 363c) (cf. Aelian, *VH* IV.8). Plutarch's account, including the subsequent reference to the Jews' supposed relation to the ass, may have been borrowed from Apion's own work—see M. Wellmann, "Aegyptisches," 242-53, and M. Stern, *Greek and Latin Authors*, no. 259.

passage—apparently decided to "improve" the Greek version of this passage (LXX Isa 19:18), by renaming the city πόλις ασεδεκ, effectively equating it with the "City of Righteousness" of Isa 1:26. Their Jewish opponents, however, were not above tampering with the biblical text themselves, and while our earliest manuscript, 1QIsᵃ, still preserves the original reading of Isa 19:18—עיר החרס ("the City of the Sun")—all the later manuscripts read עיר ההרס ("the City of Destruction") or עיר החרם ("the City of Anathema") instead.[17] Moreover, in Ezek 30:17 Heliopolis' Hebrew name is vocalized as *Awen* instead of the usual *On*—a trifle change of punctuation, perhaps, but a deliberate one nonetheless, clearly meant to equate Heliopolis with "the House of *Awen*," the derogatory name given to the shrine of Bethel (cf. Hos 4:15; 5:8; 10:5, 8).[18] This and similar puns on Heliopolis' name are also evident in several post-biblical onomastic lists, where we find entries such as "Heliopolis, in Hebrew *On*, which is affliction."[19]

How aware the Oniad Jews were of their opponents' counter-offensive we cannot tell, but there is little doubt that they did not limit their own textual efforts to Isa 19:18 alone. To legitimize their presence in Heliopolis they had to prove that they were well rooted in that city, and one way of doing so was by interpolating the Greek text of Exod 1:11. To Pithom and Raamses—the two cities built by the enslaved Jews under a wicked Pharaoh—a third was now added: "and On, which is Heliopolis (καὶ Ὤν, ἥ ἐστιν Ἡλίου πόλις)."[20] But this minor textual surgery was far from sufficient, and more solid evidence was needed. It was then that our author realized that Aseneth, this Heliopolitan maiden about whom very little was known (Gen 41:45), was a perfect

---

[17] See J.B. De Rossi, *Variae Lectiones*, 3:22; G.B. Gray, *A Critical and Exegetical Commentary*, 332-42; M. Delcor, "Le temple d'Onias," 201; A. van der Kooij, *Die alten Textzeugen*, 52-5.
[18] For a possible parallel—allusions to Hos 10:5 in an anti-Samaritan fragment—see H. Eshel, "The Prayer of Joseph from Qumran," 128.
[19] M.E. Stone, *Signs of the Judgement*, 139 (Armenian onomasticon); cf. F. Wutz, *Onomastica Sacra*, 677 (Onomasticon Marchalianum): Ἡλιουπολις (sic), πόνος; and Jerome's *Liber interpret. Hebr. nom.* (ed. De Lagarde, 132): "On (in Ezekiel), dolor vel moeror." Of course, it would have been more natural to derive the city's name from the homophonous Hebrew word *on* (BDB: "wealth, strength") than the allophonous *awen* (BDB: "trouble, sorrow, wickedness, idolatry").
[20] LXX Exod 1:11. The clumsiness of this interpolation was evident to Eusebius, who noted (*Onomasticon*, ed. Klostermann, 176) that the Jews could not have built Heliopolis during their stay in Egypt, as it already existed in Joseph's time (Gen 41:45).

peg on which to hang any claims for her city.[21] Moreover, by writing about Aseneth he could write about Joseph too, which would only enhance the story's potential appeal, given Joseph's great popularity among Egyptian Jews (who often named their children after him),[22] and the obvious similarities between Onias' career and his own. Finally, a story about Aseneth, Joseph, and their exploits could also include Levi, a cherished ancestor, granting him the prominence denied him in the biblical Joseph-story, a prominence he so richly deserved. This, I would argue, is how *Joseph and Aseneth* came into being.

With this interpretative framework in mind, the message of *Joseph and Aseneth* may be summarized as follows:

1) *Jews have deep roots in Heliopolis.* By the very fact of taking place in ancient Heliopolis, *Joseph and Aseneth* must have been very reassuring to its Oniad readers.[23] Of course, even their Egyptian neighbors would not deny the Jewish connection with Heliopolis, acknowledged already by the third century BCE Egyptian writer Manetho, who had described Moses himself as a former Heliopolitan priest.[24] But Onias' Egyptian neighbors tended to stress the end of the Manethonian account, which is why we read in CPJ III, 520, their lament at the Jews' arrival, that "the transgressors—*who had once been expelled from Egypt by the wrath of Isis* (πρότερον] ἐξ Αἰγύπτου ἐκβεβλημένοι κατὰ χόλον Ἴσιδος)—will inhabit Heliopolis."[25] By emphasizing the results of the Jews' previous stay in Egypt, Onias' Egyptian opponents were hoping that history will soon repeat itself, and that Helios-Re, or his worshippers, would drive the Jews out once

---

[21] Cf. D. Mendels, *The Land of Israel*, 34, discussing Onias' temple: "One should remember that the 'holy' places dedicated to Yahweh outside the land of Israel had no history at that time; they were not associated with any of the famous biblical sites and personalities." It is precisely this problem that *Joseph and Aseneth* addresses.

[22] See JIGRE 1 (CIJ 1427, Alexandria); 12 (Alexandria); 110 (CIJ 1485, Demerdash); 132 (provenance unknown); P.J. Sijpesteijn, "Inscriptions," 122-3 (Tell-el-Yahoudieh?); cf. V. Tcherikover, CPJ 1:30.

[23] For Heliopolis' supposed Jewish past, cf. Artapanus, frag. 2, and Ps-Eupolemus, frag. 1.

[24] *Apud* Josephus, *Ag.Ap.* I.238 (Waddell, LCL *Manetho*, fr. 54). Cf. also Apion's statement—perhaps influenced by the Oniad presence in Heliopolis—that Moses had built Jewish prayer-houses in that city (*Ag.Ap.* II.10, with M. Stern, *Greek and Latin Authors*, no. 164).

[25] G. Bohak, "CPJ III, 520," 39

again. By depicting an ancient Heliopolis where Jews lived peacefully with the local high priest and were admired by the king, *Joseph and Aseneth* implied that history actually was on the Jews' side. Moreover, having received large tracts of land in the Heliopolite nome, the Oniad Jews could claim that this land had been theirs all along—it was Aseneth's "field of inheritance" that they were now reclaiming as their own. Finally, *Joseph and Aseneth*'s author and readers may even have identified the remains of Aseneth's tower underneath their own temple, and used this identification to deflate their detractors' claims that their temple had been built over an old, impure Egyptian shrine.

2) *Onias' actions were foretold long ago.* This was a valuable argument against Onias' Jewish detractors, who claimed, as Josephus would two centuries later, that he had built his temple "not out of pure motives, but because of his rivalry with the Jews of Jerusalem, against whom he bore a grudge for his exile (οὐ μὴν Ὀνίας ἐξ ὑγιοῦς γνώμης ταῦτα ἔπραττεν, ἀλλ᾽ ἦν αὐτῷ φιλονεικία πρὸς τοὺς ἐν τοῖς Ἱεροσολύμοις Ἰουδαίους ὀργὴν τῆς φυγῆς ἀπομνημονεύοντι).''[26] But how could one claim that it was Onias' wounded ego which led to the erection of his temple, if the angel had foretold that event so many centuries earlier? In fact, not only did he foretell this event, he also showed it to result not from their own whim or fancy, but from his explicit command to the bee-priests ("Come," 16:17y). He even foretold the opposition to this move among some of the other bee-priests, and described their failed attempt to harm Aseneth. Finally, he showed Aseneth how the original honeycomb-temple, the one in Jerusalem, will be consumed by a great fire, leaving only one temple, the one in Heliopolis, as God's true shrine. For its Oniad readers, this would have been an extremely powerful message.

3) *Aseneth's "City of Refuge" would last forever.* As noted in Chapter 5.1, *Joseph and Aseneth* repeatedly refers to the eschatological "City of Refuge," in which "the sons of God" and "many nations" will dwell. God's plan, as foretold by Isaiah, to establish a Jewish temple in Egypt and bring the Egyptians to His worship was being fulfilled, and the new temple was destined to last forever (cf. LXX Isa 19:20). Those who dwell

---

[26] *War* VII.431. Josephus' negative assessment of Onias' actions is also evident in *Ant.* XIII.69, where he refers to it as a "sin (ἁμαρτία)" and "a transgression of the Torah (τοῦ νόμου παράβασις).'' The rabbis too depicted Onias the temple-builder as a vainglorious fool (b *Menahot* 109b).

around it—born Jews as well as Gentiles who repented of their idolatry—were destined to be written in "the book of the living" and to enter that heavenly "place of rest" that God and Repentance have prepared.

These, then, are the main components of *Joseph and Aseneth*'s message for its Oniad readers. While the acceptance of converts was part of that message, it was not the novel's main theme; indeed, it was merely a a by-product, as it were, of the author's belief that it was in the Heliopolitan Land of Onias that the ancient promises of the conversion of the Gentiles were soon to be fulfilled.

6.5. The Wider Literary Context

To end our discussion of *Joseph and Aseneth*'s original *Sitz im Leben*, we may now turn to one final question, namely, why would a Heliopolitan Jew choose to buttress his community's sense of legitimacy by writing a biblicizing novel? Before attempting an answer, however, we must first admit how lucky we are that he chose to do so, for were it not for his success in creating an appealing story, *Joseph and Aseneth* would not have been preserved. It is only because its later readers found it so attractive—and had no idea of its origins—that this piece of Oniad literature survived the vicissitudes of time to reach our source-thirsty eyes. This is, of course, a possible clue as to why the author chose to write a novel—novels are effective, because they are such fun to read. By writing an attractive novel, he was securing his readers' attention; by giving it a distinct biblical flavor, he was assuring their respect as well.

Yet this is only half the answer. The second half is that he chose such a vehicle to convey his message because this was precisely what so many of his contemporaries were doing. In his world, as in our own, telling stories about the past was one way of making statements about the present. Thus, although only a fraction of the Jewish literature of the Greco-Roman period has survived, there is abundant evidence that the production of new stories about the biblical heroes and their activities was a pervasive feature of the time. If one was sufficiently motivated, one could concoct fanciful stories about Abraham's close ties with the people of Sparta or Pergamon, Jacob's appointment of Levi as a priest, Moses' contribution to Egyptian zoolatry, Nehemiah's discovery of the remains of the temple's sacred fire, or Jeremiah's endorsement of Judas' leadership.[27] In some cases, the socio-political implications of these fabricated stories are not too hard to detect—a fact which, we may note, does not seem to have bothered their producers or consumers. In other cases, however, it is mainly by comparing several stories—stemming from different groups and serving conflicting agendas—that we can detect the stories' possible implications for their early users, and sense the intensity of the debates which generated them.

One of the major issues in the history of the Jewish people in the second century BCE was the controversy over which, if any, of the existing Jewish temples was legitimate. This multi-faceted dispute, which largely subsided by the end of the second century BCE, has left only a few direct traces in our sources.[28] But the various attempts to support the rival claims of several centers of Jewish allegiance also engendered the creation, or reworking, of numerous stories about the biblical Patriarchs—some of which outlived the debate itself. Naturally, the preservation of such stories is far from homogeneous, with stories emanating from Jerusalem—the side that ultimately won—surviving in greater numbers than those of any other center. Sometimes, however, enough has survived to allow us a glimpse of the process whereby such stories were generated.[29]

One interesting example of how this temple-debate unfolded is the post-biblical fate of the story of Abraham's visit to Melchizedek, king of Shalem and priest of the Most High God. From the original story (Gen 14:18-20), one cannot ascertain Shalem's geographic location, nor does the biblical narrator seem to have been much preoccupied by this issue. His later readers, however, spent much time and ingenuity in their attempts to identify Melchizedek's abode, so as to claim him—and his

---

[27] Abraham and Sparta/Pergamon: 1 Macc 12:1-23; Josephus, *Ant.* XII.225-7; XIII.164-70; XIV.255; Levi's priesthood: *Jub.* 30:18-20; 31:13-7; 32:1-9; Moses and zoolatry: Artapanus, frag. 3; Nehemiah and the fire: 2 Macc 1:18-36; Jeremiah and Judas: 2 Macc 15:12-6.

[28] See esp. *Ant.* XIII.74-79 (cf. XII.10), and the Samaritan inscriptions from Delos publilshed by Ph. Bruneau, "Les Israélites de Délos," with U. Rappaport, "The Samaritan Sect." For anti-Samaritan sentiments in the second century BCE, see, e.g., H. Eshel, "The Prayer of Joseph," 129-34, but cf. S. Schwartz, "John Hyrcanus," for a different view.

[29] In what follows, I have left out the many retellings of the Shechem story of Gen 34 (including *Joseph and Aseneth* 23:2, 14). These *may* have had an anti-Samaritan overtone (as argued by, e.g., J.J. Collins, "The Epic of Theodotus"), but cf. the cogent objections to this interpretation raised by R. Pummer, "Genesis 34."

"eternal priesthood" (Ps 110:4)—as "forerunners," as it were, of this or that cultic center. Jewish tradition plausibly identified Shalem with Jerusalem (Yeru-Shalem), an identification evident already in Ps 76:3, and further stressed in the so-called *Genesis Apocryphon*, which describes Abraham's visit to "Shalem, which is Jerusalem" (22.13). Yet this identification did not go uncontested, for another biblical verse, Gen 33:18 ("On his journey from Padan-Aram, Jacob came to Shalem, the city of Shechem in Canaan"), clearly implies that Shalem was located not in Judea, but rather in Shechemite territory.[30] This could lead to a plausible identification of the biblical Shalem with Mount Gerizim, and the Samaritans were quick to appropriate Melchizedek's city as their own:

> (Abraham) was hosted by the city at the temple Argarizin (ξενισθῆναί τε αὐτὸν ὑπὸ πόλεως ἱερὸν Ἀργαριζίν), which means "Mountain of the Most High." He also received gifts from Melchizedek who was a priest of God and a king as well.[31]

In this version of the story—erroneously attributed to the Jerusalemite writer Eupolemus—it was on Mount Gerizim that Melchizedek used to serve the Most High God. Melchizedek's priesthood, according to this account, shed its aura of antiquity and sanctity not on the Jerusalem temple, but on the rival shrine on Mount Gerizim.[32]

While each side claimed Melchizedek's sanctuary as its own, both came up with even more stories. The real Eupolemus, a protégé of Judas Maccabeus, rewrote several chapters of biblical history, stressing not only the Jews' glorious past, but also Jerusalem's centrality therein.[33]

---

[30] The LXX translation Καὶ ἦλθεν Ιακωβ εἰς Σαλημ πόλιν Σικιμων, as well as *Jub.* 30:1 (cf. Jdt 4:4), clearly support the identification of Shalem in Samaritan territory. Modern commentators postulate two homonymous locations—Jerusalem, and a second Shalem not far from Shechem (cf. B.-Z. Wacholder, "Pseudo-Eupolemus," 106). Traditional Jewish commentators often solved the problem by interpreting the word *shalem* in Gen 33:18 not as a place-name but an adjective, modifying the subject, Jacob, and meaning "complete, sound in body."

[31] For the Greek text, and the textual difficulties, see C.R. Holladay, *Fragments*, 1:172-3, and 183 n. 21.

[32] For Abraham's supposed connection with Mount Gerizim, see further B.-Z. Wacholder, *ibid.*; M. Stern, *Greek and Latin Authors*, no. 548.

[33] For the identity of Eupolemus the historian with Judas' emissary (1 Macc 8:17; 2 Macc 4:11), see, e.g., Y. Gutman, *Beginnings*, 75-8; B.-Z. Wacholder, *Eupolemus*, 1-21; Schürer (rev.), *History*, 3:518. For his political agenda, see esp. D. Mendels, *The Land of Israel*, 29-46—but note that the Leontopolite nome mentioned by Eupolemus (*ibid.*, 43, n. 52) probably refers to the real Leontopolis (Tell-Muqdam), and has nothing to do with Onias' temple.

Others embellished the biblical story of Sarah's encounter with the Egyptian king (Gen 12:10-20) by stating that the distressed Abraham had prayed to God at the very same spot on which the Jerusalem temple would later stand, and that it was due to the king's awe of this spot that Sarah had been saved (*War* V.379-81). The Samaritans, on the other hand, told a story of Moses' hiding of the sacred vessels on Mount Gerizim, a story which eventually occasioned a Samaritan disturbance, brutally crushed by the Romans (*Ant.* XVIII.85-7)—a sober reminder of the grave consequences such stories could entail.

These few glimpses of the process whereby Jerusalem's supporters and those of Mount Gerizim produced stories demonstrating their respective centers' antiquity and legitimacy may serve as a backdrop to our analysis of *Joseph and Aseneth*'s origins. When the Jerusalemites extolled their city's past glories and described Abraham's activities there, when the Samaritans told stories of Abraham's visit to Mount Gerizim and Moses' activities there, a Heliopolitan Jew came up with a story about Aseneth, Joseph, and Levi—a story set in ancient Heliopolis. He described, in vivid colors and great detail, Aseneth's repentance, the vision she was shown, the promises made to her, and her adventures as Joseph's wife. The end-product of his efforts, *Joseph and Aseneth*, is not any worse—neither in the plausibility of its claims nor in the artistry of its narrative—than the preserved fragments of Eupolemus' or Pseudo-Eupolemus' fictional histories. In fact, the case could be made that it is precisely *Joseph and Aseneth*'s literary superiority that ensured its survival. Whereas this novel was preserved as a work of literature, other works, of lesser literary merit, were neglected. The fragments thereof that we do possess we owe mainly to the diligence of Alexander Polyhistor, who mined such works for their supposed historical contents, and to Josephus, Clement, and Eusebius, who used these fragments in their discussions of ancient Jewish history.[34] From our own perspective, of course, none of these accounts of the Patriarchs' lives has any historical value with regards to the events they purport to describe. Yet there is much that they can tell us about the needs and desires of the persons or groups who composed them. The patient historian who sifts through these artificial fabrications does not go unrewarded.

---

[34] For Polyhistor's work, see esp. A. Freudenthal, *Alexander Polyhistor*; Schürer (rev.), *History*, 3:510-2.

6.6. Subsequent History

Having examined *Joseph and Aseneth*'s original *Sitz im Leben*, we may now turn to its subsequent history. This subject generally lies outside the scope of the present study, yet one episode in the novel's transmission-history deserves special mention.[35]

When we search for *Joseph and Aseneth*'s earliest readers, the evidence is extremely scanty—not surprising, perhaps, for an Oniad text, intended mainly for "internal" consumption. Only in the late fourth century CE do we find the first sign that some people were familiar, at least indirectly, with the novel. The evidence comes from the pen of a Christian pilgrim, Egeria, who visited Heliopolis ca. 382 CE:[36]

> Heliopolis lies twelve miles from Babylon. In the city's center there is a large field with the temple of the Sun, and Petefres' house is there. Between Petefres' house and the temple is Asennec's house. The inner wall within the city is very old and made of stone (surrounding?) only the temple with Asennec's house and Petefres' house.[37] In that place there is also a garden of the Sun, where there is a large column, called "Bomos," where the Phoenix used to settle after five hundred years.[38]

In his analysis of Egeria's account, Burchard correctly notes that behind this passage probably lie some traditions based on, or connected with, *Joseph and Aseneth*.[39] The fact that Pentefres had been a priest in Heliopolis would have been known to any reader of Genesis, and stories

---

[35] For *Joseph and Aseneth*'s many historical contexts, see Ch. Burchard, *Untersuchungen*, 24-45, 133-40, and esp. *id.*, "Der jüdische Asenethroman," 544-667.

[36] This section of Egeria's account is not preserved in the one extant manuscript of her travelogue, but is embedded in a twelfth-century compilation, Peter the Deacon's *Liber de Locis Sanctis*. See J. Wilkinson, *Egeria's Travels*, 204-5 and Ch. Burchard, *Untersuchungen*, 137-8; *id.*, "Der jüdische Asenethroman," 554-6.

[37] My translation follows Geyer and Burchard in assuming that a word (iungens? includens?) is missing before *tantummodo*. Cf. J. Wilkinson's translation: "The inner wall of the city is of a considerable age, as old as the temple, or the houses of Asenath and Potiphar, and like them it is made of stone" (*Egeria's Travels*, 204).

[38] Petrus Diaconus, ed. Geyer, 115: "Eliopolis distat a Babilonia milia duodecim. In medio autem huius civitatis est campus ingens, in quo est templum Solis, et ibi est domus Petefrae. Inter domum autem Petefrae et templum est domus Asennec. Murus autem interior intra civitatem est antiquior lapideusque * tantummodo templum cum domo Asennec et domo Petefrae. Ibi vero est et viridarium Solis, ubi columna est grandis, quae appellatur Bomon, in qua Phoenix post quingentos annos residere consuevit."

[39] Ch. Burchard, *Untersuchungen*, 137-8; "Der jüdische Asenethroman," 554-6.

about his Heliopolitan house could have developed among people who never read *Joseph and Aseneth*. But the fact that there were two houses, Pentefres' house and next to it a separate house for Aseneth, is never mentioned in any other source. This, and Egeria's reference to a garden lying next to Aseneth's house, and to the stone wall surrounding the whole complex, probably should be taken as signs of some familiarity in fourth-century Heliopolis with traditions connected with *Joseph and Aseneth* (cf. esp. 2:10-2). Egeria's guides may have been Jews, a small remnant of the pre-Hadrianic community, but are more likely to have been local Christians, dimly aware of older Heliopolitan traditions.[40] Egeria herself, to be sure, never mentions Onias' temple, which would have been of very little interest to her anyway.[41] She was searching for sites connected with biblical figures, such as the thrones of Moses and Aaron, the granaries of Joseph, and "the village where holy Mary stayed with the Lord when she went to Egypt."[42] Onias' temple was of no interest to her, no more than the schools of Plato and Eudoxus, which had so fired Strabo's imagination (*Geog.* XVII.1.29), and which she utterly ignored. As often is the case, what pilgrims see is what they came to see.

Egeria's account provides the earliest known evidence of any person's familiarity with *Joseph and Aseneth*, and lends further support to the suggestion of an intimate connection between the novel and Heliopolis itself. Shortly afterward, this ancient novel was discovered by quite a few readers, for several fifth-century Saints' lives are known that show an unmistakable dependence upon it.[43] In the next century, we hear of an old Greek book found in the library of an episcopal Syrian family and sent to Moses of Aggel for translation and interpretation— the request with which the present study began. How and when the book made its way from Egypt to Syria and Asia Minor we may never know,

---

[40] For the Christian presence in Heliopolis see, e.g., John Moschos, *Pratum Spirituale*, 124; E. Amélineau, *La géographie de l'Égypte*, 287-8; S. Timm, *Christlische-koptische Ägypten*, 910-4; 1613-20.
[41] If Egeria's guides indeed were pointing to the structure described in *Joseph and Aseneth*, and if our suggestion in Chapter 4.2.5 is correct, she may even have been at the place where Onias' temple once stood. For her mention of the βωμός (altar) and the Phoenix, cf. Bartholomaeus Anglicus' *De Proprietatibus Rerum* XII.14—a thirteenth century description of the bird's arrival on Onias' altar—with R. van den Broek, *The Myth of the Phoenix*, 117-9.
[42] See J. Wilkinson, *Egeria's Travels*, 203-4.
[43] See Ch. Burchard, *Untersuchungen*, 134-7; *id.*, "Die jüdische Asenethroman," 558-9.

but in the next few centuries it became immensely popular and was translated into numerous languages. It was rewritten several times, even in Greek, and spread throughout much of the medieval world. None of its readers had the slightest clue as to its Oniad provenance (or even its Jewish origins), and it is this ignorance, and the novel's own appeal, that assured *Joseph and Aseneth* its miraculous survival. For a book originally written by a small group whose enterprise proved a dismal failure and whose very existence was almost entirely forgotten, such remarkable tenacity is not to be despised.

Chapter 7

Conclusions and Suggestions for Further Research

Our study has reached its end. We began with a question addressed to a sixth-century bishop, Moses of Aggel, concerning an old Greek book, and ended with the fascinating world of ancient Jewish fictional histories and partisan propaganda. It is now time to briefly review our main conclusions, which differ greatly from those of *Joseph and Aseneth*'s previous modern readers:

1) *Joseph and Aseneth* was written by a Heliopolitan Jew, intimately connected with Onias' temple. It probably was written in the middle of the second century BCE, but a later date cannot be ruled out.

2) *Joseph and Aseneth*'s central scene is an apocalyptic revelation scene, in which an angel shows Aseneth, in a symbolic vision, how one day a group of Jewish priests would leave the Jerusalem temple and build an identical temple in Heliopolis, how other priests would try, and fail, to harm this project, and how the Jerusalem temple itself eventually would be destroyed.

3) *Joseph and Aseneth* is best read as a story which sought to furnish its Oniad readers with arguments in support of their settlement in Heliopolis, the erection of their temple there, and the acquisition of large tracts of neighboring territory through a Ptolemaic grant. It also sought to assure its Oniad readers that their opponents were bound to fail, and that their own "City of Refuge" would last forever, sheltering within its

wall not only "the sons of God" but also the "many nations" whose coming had been foretold by the Prophets.

Our main conclusion, then, is that instead of reading *Joseph and Aseneth* as an embarrassed reader's reaction to Gen 41:45,[1] as "a religious myth that explains the origins of proselytism,"[2] or as a work setting out "to enhance the status of Gentile converts in the Jewish community,"[3] we may read it as *a fictional history which "foretells," and justifies, the establishment of the Jewish temple in Heliopolis.*

This interpretative framework helps explain many elements in the novel that have previously remained enigmatic and obscure. There is, however, much further work to be done, both on *Joseph and Aseneth* itself and on texts and issues to which it might be related. To end this study, I would like to briefly outline some of the questions that it raises and their implications for future scholarship.

One important issue that emerges from the present study is the need to reexamine several other ancient Jewish texts for which an Oniad origin has tentatively been proposed. This is true for *2 Enoch,*[4] and even more so for the *Sibylline Oracles,* or, at least, for sections of the *Third* and *Fifth Sibylline Oracles.*[5] Unfortunately, these texts share two traits in common—an obscure transmission history and a corrupt textual tradition—qualities which often hamper the thorough analysis of their contents and meanings. In spite of these difficulties, however, a fresh examination of their possible connections with Onias' temple, based in part on detailed comparisons with *Joseph and Aseneth,* would yield new and fruitful insights.

Another promising venue would be a detailed comparison of *Joseph and Aseneth* with the Egyptian literary tradition, and especially Egyptian fiction of the Greco-Roman period. This is a scholarly road not yet taken, a road that could lead—as noted in Chapter 4.2.1-2—to many important discoveries. It is also a road that anyone interested in the history of the Greek novel as a whole eventually will be forced to take.[6]

---

[1] A. Momigliano, *Alien Wisdom,* 117-8; Burchard, "Joseph and Aseneth," 177.
[2] G.W.E. Nickelsburg, *Jewish Literature,* 262.
[3] R.D. Chesnutt, *From Death to Life,* 264.
[4] See U. Fischer, *Eschatologie,* 40 and M. Philonenko, *Joseph et Aséneth,* 60, 167-8.
[5] See J.J. Collins, *The Sibylline Oracles,* 52-3. with A. Chester's reservations ("The Sibyl," 41-3).
[6] See J.W.B. Barns, "Egypt and the Greek Romance," and, most recently, F. Hoffmann, *Ägypter und Amazonen,* 29.

In addition to these literary analyses, the present study clearly demonstrates the need for a fresh look at the historical episode of Onias' temple. Unfortunately, previous studies focused primarily on the issue of this temple's "importance" vis-à-vis Jerusalem, with different scholars using the same (meager) evidence to arrive at diametrically opposed conclusions. Some insisted that Onias' "schismatic" temple posed a major challenge to the one in Jerusalem, and to Jewish unity as a whole.[7] Others denied it any historical significance, and ridiculed the notion of an Oniad challenge to Jerusalem's supremacy.[8] Much of this debate, though by no means all of it, raged around the festal letters of 2 Macc 1:1-2:18—letters that never mention Onias' temple, and patently lend themselves to more than one interpretation. Reexamining this debate, one cannot avoid noting hypotheses and conclusions determined solely by preconceived notions of what ancient Jews must have been like, or of what modern Jews should be like. Moreover, the very terms of reference used—and especially the notion of a "schism"—have often been colored by misguided perceptions of the Jews' internal conflicts in the Greco-Roman period. Finally, it must be stressed that both the excessive insistence on Onias' temple as a constant challenge to Jerusalem's authority and the complete denial of that challenge have led scholarship astray. Thus, one sad effect of Tcherikover's oft-repeated dictum that "in the whole of Judaeo-Alexandrian literature there is no trace of Onias' temple"[9] was that the possibility of a connection between that temple and a text such as *Joseph and Aseneth*, entirely devoted to Heliopolis' Jewish past, was utterly ignored. In similar fashion, an Egyptian "prophecy" that expressly mentions the Jews' return to Heliopolis was read by numerous scholars who failed to see its possible relevance for the study of the Land of Onias.[10] Yet the opposite claim, that Onias' temple cast a giant shadow over the Judean hills, was no more helpful, for it led scholars to read far too many works as somehow

---

[7] E.g., U. Kahrstedt, *Syrische Territorien*, 132-45; A. Momigliano, *Prime linee*, 93-4; *id.*, "La portata storica," 1078-9; E. Bickerman "Ein jüdischer Festbrief", 154, n. 60; E. Cavaignac, "Remarques," 42-58; J.A. Goldstein, *I Maccabees*, 546-50; *id.*, *II Maccabees*, 24-6.
[8] E.g., R. Doran, *Temple Propaganda*, 11-2; A. Kasher, "Political and National Connections," 31-2; J.J. Collins, *Between Athens and Jerusalem*, 78-9; R. Yankelevitch, "The Temple of Onias."
[9] V. Tcherikover, *Hellenistic Civilization*, 278; cf. *id.*, CPJ 1:45.
[10] G. Bohak, "CPJ III, 520," 32-3.

connected with, or aimed against, that temple.[11] Finding Onias' temple between the lines of every ancient Jewish text is as misleading as not finding it at all.

In light of such errors, it seems that the question of Heliopolis' "importance" vis-à-vis Jerusalem, intriguing (and relevant) as it may be to a modern audience, is not the right question to ask. Instead, we must make another concentrated effort at locating all the traces that Onias' temple may have left in our sources. Not only must we carefully reread such texts as 2 *Enoch* and the *Sibylline Oracles*, we must also pay close attention to the many Jewish, Christian, and Muslim traditions about the Patriarchs' activities in the Heliopolis-Memphis region, to see whether they might originally have been influenced by the Jewish presence there.[12] Finally, we must examine all the Egyptian texts of the Greco-Roman period that mention Heliopolis, to find out whether their attitudes to that city reflect its contemporary historical situation.

Sifting through all these texts, isolating the relevant traditions, and assessing their possible Oniad connection is a daunting task, but one we must not shy away from—to reconstruct the lives of history's losers, historians often must search through some very odd dust bins. This is a time-consuming and often thankless enterprise, but we must not give up the search before it has begun, nor pronounce a verdict before assembling all the evidence. The Land of Onias, with its several Jewish settlements clustered around their temple, is a fascinating episode in ancient Jewish history, and it deserves a full, unbiased scrutiny. In the study of the past we must show empathy for all, and sympathy to none—for if we fail to strive for this unattainable goal, our own historical work soon turns out to have been just one more piece of fictional history and partisan propaganda.

---

[11] See, e.g., A. Momigliano's reading of the *Let. Arist.* ("Per la data"), occasionally resuscitated by later scholars, J.A. Goldstein's reconstruction of an "Oniad Saga" supposedly written by Onias IV ("The Tales of the Tobiads;" *I Maccabees*, 57-9; *II Maccabees*, 35-7), or R.T. White's interpretation of the Dead Sea Scrolls ("The House of Peleg"). Cf. E. Bammel, "Das Judentum," 9-10.

[12] Some useful starting points may be found in E. Amélineau, *Géographie*, 246-7, 287-8; Maspero-Wiet, *Matériaux*, 131-2; 208-9; R.H. Stricker, "La prison de Joseph," 101-37; D.G. Jeffreys, *The Survey of Memphis*, 1:55-6 ("Joseph toponyms in the Memphite area"); A.-P. Zivie, "Du côté de Babylone," 511-7, and *id.*, "Du bon usage," 303-4; S. Timm, *Christliche-koptische Ägypten*, 910-5; 1612-20 etc.

Appendix 1

The Textual History of *Joseph and Aseneth*

As noted in the Introduction, *Joseph and Aseneth* has come down to us in four different recensions. Throughout our study, we focused on one of these, represented by the manuscript family *b*. It is time to turn to the other recensions of our novel.

One of these recensions, represented by the manuscript family *a*, generally resembles our recension in its contents and differs from it mainly in language and style. It tries, for example, to avoid the constant parataxis that characterizes the *b* text by using participle-constructions instead, or replacing a καὶ with another particle, such as δὲ or οὖν. As noted by Burchard, Philonenko, and others, such variations clearly reflect a conscious attempt to "improve" the novel's biblicizing Greek. Thus, *a* must be considered a deliberate, and relatively late, revision of *Joseph and Aseneth*.[1] Another recension, represented by the manuscript family *c*, breaks off in the middle of the honeycomb scene and omits the last third of our novel.[2] On stylistic grounds, however, it too has been shown to be a late revision of our text.[3]

The fourth recension, represented by manuscript family *d*, is where the real debate begins. It is very similar to the *b* text in its vocabulary and style, but is about one third shorter. In Burchard's view, recension *b* is closer to the original text and *d* is a later abridgment. Philonenko, on

---

[1] Ch. Burchard, *Untersuchungen*, 19-22; *id.*, "The Present State," 32-4; M. Philonenko, *Joseph et Aséneth*, 4-6.
[2] One manuscript, H, adds a new ending, down to 21:9, in Modern Greek.
[3] Ch. Burchard, "The Present State," 33-4; M. Philonenko, *Joseph et Aséneth*, 9-11.

the other hand, sees *d* as closer to the original, with the *b* text representing a later, expanded edition.[4]

The present study can, in my view, shed new light on this question. Naturally, our findings thus far apply to recension *b* only, and cannot automatically decide the question of the relationship between *b* and *d*. On the one hand, it is possible that an Oniad text, of which *b* is the best witness we have, was abridged at some later stage, and this abridged version is what we find in *d*; on the other hand, it is equally possible that an Oniad author took an existing narrative, which looked more or less like *d*, and expanded it into the *b* text, to better suit his particular needs. However, when the two texts are placed side by side, *d* is clearly seen to be an abridged text, produced by someone who had no notion of what *Joseph and Aseneth* originally was all about. To see this clearly, we may examine one passage as an example, the crucial passage at the heart of the honeycomb scene (16:17y-17:2). To highlight the differences between the two texts we print them side-by-side and translate the text of the shorter recension, *d*:

b (Burchard's text):[5]	*d* (Philonenko's text):[6]
Καὶ ἀνέστησαν μέλισσαι ἐκ τῶν σίμβλων τοῦ κηρίου ἐκείνου καὶ οἱ σίμβλοι ἦσαν ἀναρίθμητοι μυριάδες μυριάδων καὶ χιλιάδες χιλιάδων. Καὶ ἦσαν αἱ μέλισσαι λευκαὶ ὡσεὶ χιὼν καὶ τὰ πτερὰ αὐτῶν ὡς πορφύρα καὶ ὡς ὑάκινθος καὶ ὡς κόκκος καὶ ὡς βύσσινα ἱμάτια χρυσοϋφῆ	Καὶ ἀνέβησαν μέλισσαι ἐκ τῶν σίμβλων τοῦ κηρίου
	καὶ ἦσαν λευκαὶ ὡσεὶ χιὼν καὶ αἱ πτέρυγες αὐτῶν ὡς πορφύρα καὶ ὡς ὑάκινθος
	καὶ ὡσεὶ νήματα χρυσοῦ
καὶ διαδήματα χρυσᾶ ἐπὶ τὰς κεφαλὰς αὐτῶν καὶ κέντρα ἦσαν αὐταῖς ὀξέα καὶ οὐκ ἠδίκουν τινά. Καὶ περιεπλάκησαν πᾶσαι αἱ μέλισσαι ἐκεῖναι τῇ Ἀσενὲθ	καὶ ἦσαν διαδήματα χρυσᾶ ἐπὶ τὰς κεφαλὰς αὐτῶν καὶ κέντρα ὀξέα. Καὶ συνεπλάκησαν πᾶσαι αἱ μέλισσαι τῇ Ἀσενὲθ

4 Ch. Burchard, *Untersuchungen*, 19-23; *id.*, "Zum Text," 18-28; M. Philonenko, *Joseph et Aséneth*, 9-11.
5 Ch. Burchard, "Ein vorläufiger griechischer Text," 29-30.
6 M. Philonenko, *Joseph et Aséneth*, 188-90.

ἀπὸ ποδῶν ἕως κεφαλῆς.
καὶ ἄλλαι μέλισσαι ἦσαν μεγάλαι
καὶ ἐκλεκταὶ ὡς βασίλισσαι αὐτῶν
καὶ ἐξανέστησαν ἀπὸ τῆς πληγῆς
τοῦ κηρίου καὶ περιεπλάκησαν περὶ
τὸ πρόσωπον Ἀσενὲθ καὶ ἐποίησαν
ἐπὶ τῷ στόματι αὐτῆς καὶ ἐπὶ τὰ
χείλη αὐτῆς κηρίον ὅμοιον τῷ
κηρίῳ τῷ παρακειμένῳ τῷ
ἀνθρώπῳ.
Καὶ πᾶσαι αἱ μέλισσαι ἐκεῖναι
ἤσθιον ἀπὸ τοῦ κηρίου τοῦ ὄντος
ἐπὶ τῷ στόματι Ἀσενὲθ.
Καὶ εἶπεν ὁ ἄνθρωπος ταῖς
μελίσσαις· ὑπάγετε δὴ εἰς τὸν
τόπον ὑμῶν. Καὶ ἀνέστησαν πᾶσαι
αἱ μέλισσαι καὶ ἐπετάσθησαν
καὶ ἀπῆλθον εἰς τὸν οὐρανὸν.
Καὶ ὅσαι ἠβουλήθησαν ἀδικῆσαι
    τὴν Ἀσενὲθ
ἔπεσον ἐπὶ τὴν γῆν
καὶ ἀπέθανον. Καὶ ἐξέτεινεν
ὁ ἄνθρωπος τὴν ῥάβδον αὐτοῦ
ἐπὶ τὰς μελίσσας τὰς νεκρὰς
καὶ εἶπεν αὐταῖς· ἀνάστητε
καὶ ὑμεῖς καὶ ἀπέλθετε
εἰς τὸν τόπον ὑμῶν.
Καὶ ἀνέστησαν
αἱ τεθνηκυῖαι μέλισσαι
καὶ ἀπῆλθον   εἰς
τὴν αὐλὴν τὴν παρακειμένην
τῇ οἰκίᾳ τῆς Ἀσενέθ
καὶ ἐσκήνωσαν ἐπὶ τοῖς δένδροις
τοῖς καρποφόροις.
Καὶ εἶπεν ὁ ἄνθρωπος τῇ Ἀσενέθ·
ἑώρακας τὸ ῥῆμα τοῦτο;
καὶ αὐτὴ εἶπεν· ναί, κύριε,
ἑώρακα ταῦτα πάντα.
Καὶ εἶπεν αὐτῇ ὁ ἄνθρωπος·

ἀπὸ ποδῶν ἕως κεφαλῆς.
καὶ ἄλλαι μέλισσαι   μεγάλαι
                ὡς βασίλισσαι

                ἐκράτησαν
        τῇ Ἀσενὲθ
                ἐπὶ τὰ
χείλη.

Καὶ εἶπεν ὁ ἄνθρωπος ταῖς
μελίσσαις· ὑπάγετε δὴ εἰς τοὺς
τόπους ὑμῶν. Καὶ ἀπῆλθον πᾶσαι

ἀπὸ τῆς Ἀσενὲθ καὶ
ἔπεσαν ἐπὶ τὴν γῆν πᾶσαι
καὶ ἀπέθανον.

Καὶ εἶπεν ὁ ἄνθρωπος· ἀνάστητε
δὴ   καὶ ἀπέλθατε
εἰς τὸν τόπον ὑμῶν.
Καὶ ἀνέστησαν

καὶ ἀπῆλθον ἅπασαι πρὸς
τὴν αὐλὴν τὴν παρακειμένην
τῇ   Ἀσενέθ.

Καὶ εἶπεν ὁ ἄνθρωπος τῇ Ἀσενέθ·
ἑώρακας τὸ ῥῆμα τοῦτο;
καὶ   εἶπεν· ἰδοὺ ἐγώ, κύριε,
ἑώρακα ταῦτα πάντα.
Καὶ εἶπεν   ὁ ἄνθρωπος·

οὕτως ἔσται πάντα   οὕτως ἔσται
τὰ ῥήματά μου ἃ λελάληκα   τὰ ῥήματα   ἃ ἐλάλησα
πρός σε σήμερον·   πρὸς σέ.

> And bees went up from the cells of the comb, and the bees were white as snow, and their wings like purple and like violet and like threads of gold, and they had golden diadems on their heads, and (they had) sharp stings. And all the bees converged on Aseneth from her feet to her head. And other bees, as large as queens, took over Aseneth's lips. And the man said to the bees, "Go to your places." And they all left Aseneth and fell on the ground and died. And the man said, "Rise and go off to your place." And they all rose and went off into the court adjoining Aseneth. And the man said to Aseneth, "Have you seen this thing?" And (she) said, "indeed, Lord, I have seen all these things." And the man said, "So will be the words which I spoke to you."

The differences between the two texts are substantial, leaving us a clear choice. If we assume the priority of the *b* text, we must admit that the person responsible for the abridged version had no idea of the passage's original meaning. Otherwise, he would not have deleted the statement that "the cells were innumerable, myriads upon myriads and thousands upon thousands," a phrase with strong priestly connotations in ancient Jewish literature (cf. Chapter 1, n. #). Nor would he have deleted the scarlet and the linen from the description of the bees' appearance, effectively depriving them of their priestly quality. Moreover, whoever abridged the longer version clearly did not realize the significance of the bees' establishment of a new honeycomb on Aseneth's mouth, or of the presence of two types of bees, good and bad ones. This is why he deleted the description of their building activities, and omitted all mention of the bad bees and their fate. In his version there is only one type of bees, bees that die and then go to Aseneth's garden. Lacking a clue to the scene's true meaning, he probably found much of it too fantastic, too enigmatic, or too boring, and opted to leave it out.

If, on the other hand, we assume the priority of the shorter text, several major problems emerge. First, in Philonenko's text there is an inexplicable change from "your places" to "your place," and the phrase "the court adjoining Aseneth" also seems rather awkward.[7] Second, and

---

[7] For both points, see Ch. Burchard, "Zum Text," 20. Note, however, A. Standhartinger's objection that the longer text too is not free of narrative inconsistencies (*Das Frauenbild im Judentum*, 221-2).

more significant, there are many narrative opportunities which the shorter text seems to miss. The attempt of Joseph's bad brothers to hurt Aseneth is not foreshadowed by the bad bees' attattack, since no bad bees are ever mentioned. The importance of forgiving one's enemies, stressed throughout the text, does not play a role here, as no bees are forgiven by the angel. Levi's exalted status is not paralleled by the bees' priestly appearance, entirely absent from this version of the honeycomb scene.

There is, of course, no absolute proof that the shorter text could not have been written in this way by some unknown original author. What can be said, however, is that the burden of proof lies squarely on the shoulders of those who wish to champion d as closer to the original text. To support such a claim, one would have to come up with a suitable explanation of how and why this peculiar text was written, prior to its use by an Oniad author who expanded it into a more coherent whole. Providing such an explanation is no easy task.

Abbreviations

AGAJU	*Arbeiten zur Geschichte des Antiken Judentums und des Urchristentums*
ANRW	*Aufstieg und Niedergang der Römischen Welt*
APOT	R.H. Charles, *The Apocrypha and Pseudepigrapha of the Old Testament*, 2 vols., Oxford: Clarendon, 1913
ASAE	*Annales du Service des Antiquités de l'Egypte*
BASOR	*Bulletin of the American School of Oriental Research*
BCH	*Bulletin de Correspondance Hellénique*
BDB	F. Brown, S.R. Driver, and C.A. Briggs, *A Hebrew and English Lexicon of the Old Testament*, Oxford: Clarendon, 1906 (repr. 1951)
BIA	*Bulletin d'Information Archéologique*
BIFAO	*Bulletin de l'Institut Francais d'Archéologie Orientale*
BSAA	*Bulletin de la Société d'Archéologie d'Alexandrie*
CCSL	*Corpus Christianorum, Series Latina*
CdE	*Chronique d'Egypte*
CPJ	V. Tcherikover, A. Fuks, and M. Stern (eds.), *Corpus Papyrorum Judaicarum*, Cambridge: Harvard University Press, 3 vols., 1957-64
CQ	*Classical Quarterly*
CSCO	*Corpus Scriptorum Christianorum Orientalium*
CSEL	*Corpus Scriptorum Ecclesiasticorum Latinorum*
DHA	*Dialogues d'Histoire Ancienne*
EPRO	*Etudes Préliminaires aux Religions Orientales dans l'Empire Romain*
ET	*The Expository Times*
HTR	*Harvard Theological Review*
HUCA	*Hebrew Union College Annual*
ICS	*Illinois Classical Studies*
JBL	*Journal of Biblical Literature*
JIGRE	W. Horbury and D. Noy, *Jewish Inscriptions of Graeco-Roman Egypt*, Cambridge: Cambridge University Press, 1992
JJS	*Journal of Jewish Studies*
JNES	*Journal of Near Eastern Studies*
JRH	*Journal of Religious History*
JSHRZ	*Jüdische Schriften aus hellenistisch-römischer Zeit*
JSJ	*Journal for the Study of Judaism in the Persian, Hellenistic and Roman Periods*
JSOT	*Journal for the Study of the Old Testament*
JSNT	*Journal for the Study of the New Testament*
JTS	*Journal of Theological Studies*
LCL	*Loeb Classical Library*
LdÄ	W. Helck and E. Otto (eds.), *Lexikon der Ägyptologie*, Wiesbaden: Otto Harrassowitz, 7 vols., 1972-89
MPER	*Mitteilungen aus der Sammlung der Papyrus Erzherzog Rainer*
NT	*Novum Testamentum*
NTS	*New Testament Studies*
OTP	J.H. Charlesworth (ed.), *The Old Testament Pseudepigrapha*, Garden City: Doubleday, 2 vols., 1983-5
PAAJR	*Proceedings of the American Academy of Jewish Research*

PGM   K. Preisendanz, *Papyri Graecae Magicae*, (rev. by A. Henrichs), 2 vols., Stuttgart: Teubner, 1973-4

RB   *Revue Biblique*

RE   Pauly-Wissowa, *Realencyclopädie der classichen Altertumswissenschaft*, 1893-

RecTrav   *Recueil de travaux relatifs a la philologie et a l'archeologie Egyptiennes et Assyriens*

REJ   *Revue des Etudes Juives*

RHPhR   *Revue d'histoire et de philosophie religieuses*

RHR   *Revue de l'Histoire des Religions*

RPh   *Revue de Philologie*

RQ   *Revue de Qumran*

SAOC   *Studies in Ancient Oriental Civilization*

TAPA   *Transactions and Proceedings of the American Philological Association*

ThDNT   G. Kittel and G. Friedrich (eds.),*Theological Dictionary of the New Testament*

TSAJ   *Texte und Studien zum Antiken Judentum*

UPZ   U. Wilcken, *Urkunden der Ptolemäerzeit*, 2 vols., Berlin: De Gruyter, 1927-57

VT   *Vetus Testamentum*

WUNT   *Wissenschaftliche Untersuchungen zum Neuen Testament*

ZÄS   *Zeitschrift für Ägyptische Sprache*

ZAW   *Zeitschrift für Alttestamentliche Wissenschaft*

ZDPV   *Zeitschrift des Deutscen Palästina-Vereins*

ZNW   *Zeitschrift für Neutestamentliche Wissenschaft*

ZPE   *Zeitschrift für Papyrologie und Epigraphik*

Bibliography

F.-M. Abel, *Les livres des Maccabées*, Paris: Librairie Lecoffre, 1949

Sh. Adam, "Recent Discoveries in the Eastern Delta (Dec. 1950-May 1955)," *ASAE* 55 (1958), 301-24

B. Agnostou-Canas, "Rapports de dépendance coloniale dans l'Egypte ptolémaïque II. Les rebelles de la Chôra," in-A.H.S. El-Mosalamy (ed.), *Proceedings of the XIXth Int.ernational Congress of Papyrology*, Cairo: Ain Shams University, 1993, 2:323-72

T.G. Allen, *The Book of the Dead, or Going Forth by Day* [Studies in Ancient Oriental Civilization 37], Chicago: University of Chicago Press, 1974

G. Alon, "The Burning of the Temple," in-*id.*, *Jews, Judaism and the Classical World*, Jerusalem: Magnes, 252-68

E. Amélineau, *La géographie de l'Egypte à l'époque copte*, repr. Osnabrück: Otto Zeller, 1973 (or. ed. 1893)

V. Aptowitzer, "Asenath, the Wife of Joseph: A Haggadic Literary-Historical Study," *HUCA* 1 (1924), 239-306

D. Arenhoevel, *Die Theokratie nach dem 1. und 2. Makkabäerbuch* [Walberberger Studien der Albertus-Magnus-Akademie, Theologische Reihe 3], Mainz: Matthias-Grünewald, 1967

G. Avni, Z. Greenhut, and T. Ilan, "Three new Burial Caves from the Second Temple Period in Haqqal Damma in the Qidron Valley," *Qadmoniot* 25 (1992), 100-10 (Heb.)

C. Aziza, "L'utilization polémique du récit de l'Exode chez les écrivains alexandrins," *ANRW* II.20.1 (1987), 41-65

Baedeker's Egypt 1929, Leipzig: K. Baedeker, 1929 (repr. Newton Abbot: David & Charles, 1974)

J. Baines and J. Malek, *Atlas of Ancient Egypt*, Oxford: Phaidon, 1980

J. Ball, *Egypt in the Classical Geographers*, Cairo: Government Press, 1942

E. Bammel, "Das Judentum als eine Religion Ägyptens," in-M. Görg (ed.), *Religion im Erbe Ägyptens*, Wiesbaden: Otto Harrassowitz, 1988, 1-10

E. El-Banna, "L'Obélisque de Sésostris I à Héliopolis: A-t-il été déplacé," *RdE* 33 (1981), 4-9

J.W.B. Barns, "Egypt and the Greek Romance," in-H. Gerstinger (ed.), *Akten des VIII. internationalen Kongress für Papyrologie*, [MPER 5], Wien: Rohrer, 1956, 29-36

W. Barta, "Re," *LdÄ*, 5:156-80

A. Barucq, "Léontopolis," in-L. Pirot, A. Robert, and H. Cazelles (eds.), *Dictionnaire de la Bible*, Suppl. V, Paris: Letouzy & Ané, 1957, 359-72

G. Bastianini, "Lista dei prefetti d'Egitto dal 30ª al 299ᵖ," *ZPE* 17 (1975), 263-328

—, "Lista dei prefetti d'Egitto dal 30ª al 299ᵖ: Aggiunte e correzioni," *ZPE* 38 (1980), 75-89

—, "Il prefetto d'Egitto (30 a.C.—297 d.C.): Addenda (1973-1985)," *ANRW* II.10.1 (1988), 503-17

G. Bastianini and J. Whitehorne, *Strategi and Royal Scribes of Roman Egypt: Chronological List and Index*, [Pap. Flor. XV], Firenze: Gonnelli, 1987

P. Batiffol, *Le livre de la prière d'Aseneth*, [Studia Patristica I-II], Paris, 1889-90

R.T. Beckwith, "The Solar Calendar of Joseph and Asenath: A Suggestion," *JSJ* 15 (1984), 90-111

M.A. Beek, "Relations entre Jérusalem et la diaspora égyptienne au 2ᵉ siècle avant J.C.," *Oudtestamentlische Studien* 2 (1943), 119-143

E. Bernand, "Le culte du lion en basse Egypte d'après les monuments grecs," *DHA* 16 (1990), 63-94

—, "Au dieu très haut," in-*Hommages à Jean Cousin*, Paris: Les Belles Lettres, 1983, 107-11

E.J. Bickerman, "Ein jüdischer Festbrief vom Jahre 124 v. Chr. (II Macc. 1,1-9)," *ZNW* 32 (1933), 233-54 [repr. in-*id.*, *Studies in Jewish and Christian History*, Leiden: Brill, 1980, 2:136-58]

—, "The Warning Inscriptions of Herod's Temple," *JQR* 37 (1946/7), 387-405

—, *From Ezra to the Last of the Maccabees: Foundations of Postbiblical Judaism*, New York: Schocken, 1962

L. Bodson, *IEPA ZΩIA: Contribution à l'étude de la place de l'animal dans la religion grecque ancienne*, Bruxelles: Academie Royale de Belgique, 1975

G. Bohak, "Aseneth's Honeycomb and Onias' Temple: The Key to *Joseph and Aseneth*?," in-*Proceedings of the Eleventh World Congress of Jewish Studies*, Jerusalem: World Union of Jewish Studies, 1994, Division A, 163-170.

Bibliography   115

—, "CPJ III, 520: The Egyptian Reaction to Onias' Temple," *JSJ* 36 (1995), 32-41

—, "Good Jews, Bad Jews, and Non-Jews in Greek Papyri and Inscriptions," in-*Proceedings of the XXIst International Congress of Papyrologists (Berlin, August 13-19, 1995)*, forthcoming

—, "The Ibis and the Jewish Question: Ancient "Anti-Semitism" in Historical Perspective," in-M. Mor and A. Oppenheimer (eds.), *Jewish-Gentile Relations in the Second Temple, Mishnaic, and Talmudic Periods*, Jerusalem: Ben Zvi, forthcoming

D. Bonneau, "Les *realia* du paysage égyptien dans le roman grec: Remarques lexicographiques," in-M.-F. Baslez, P. Hoffmann, and M.Trédé (eds.), *Le monde du roman grec* [Etudes de littérature ancienne, tome 4], Paris: Presses de l'Ecole Normale Supérieure, 1992, 213-9

C. Bonner, *Studies in Magical Amulets Chiefly Graeco-Egyptian*, Ann Arbor: University of Michigan Press, 1950

J. Brand, "To the affair of Onias' temple," *Yavneh* 1 (1939), 76-84 (Heb.)

M. Braun, *History and Romance in Graeco-Oriental Literature*, Oxford: Basil Blackwell, 1938

H. Braunert, *Die Binnenwanderung: Studien zur Sozialgeschichte Ägyptens in der Ptolemäer- und Kaiserzeit* [Bonner Historische Forschungen, 26], Bonn: L. Röhrscheid, 1964

R. van den Broek, *The Myth of the Phoenix, According to Classical and Early Christian Traditions* [EPRO 24], Leiden: E.J. Brill, 1972

E.W. Brooks, *Historia Ecclesiastica Zachariae Rhetori vulgo adscripta*: *Textus*, CSCO 83, Paris, 1919, *Versio*, CSCO 87, Louvain, 1924

B.J. Brooten, *Women Leaders in the Ancient Synagogue: Inscriptional Evidence and Background Issues* [Brown Judaic Studies 36], Chico: Scholars Press, 1982

E. Brugsch-Bey, "On et Onion," *RecTrav* 8 (1886), 1-9

Ph. Bruneau, "Les Israélites de Délos et la juiverie délienne," *BCH* 106 (1982), 465-504

J.G. Bunge, *Untersuchungen zum 2 Makkabäeräbuch*, Bonn: Rheinische Friedrich-Wilhelms-Universität, 1971

—, "Zur Geschichte und Chronologie des Unterganges der Oniaden und des Aufstiegs der Hamonäer," *JSJ* 6 (1975), 1-46

Ch. Burchard, *Untersuchungen zu Joseph und Aseneth*, (WUNT 8), Tübingen: J.C.B. Mohr, 1965

—, *Der dreizehnte Zeuge: Traditions- und kompositions-geschichtlische Untersuchungen zu Lukas' Darstellung der Frühzeit des Paulus*, Göttingen: Vandenhoeck & Ruprecht, 1970

—, "Zum Text von 'Joseph und Aseneth'," *JSJ* 1 (1970), 3-34

—, "Joseph et Aséneth: Questions actuelles," in-W.C. van Unnik (ed.), *La littérature juive entre Tenach et Mischna: Quelques problèms*, Leiden: E.J. Brill, 1974, 77-100

—, "Ein vorläufiger griechischer Text von Joseph und Aseneth," *Dielheimer Blätter zum Alten Testament* 14 (1979), 2-53, with corrections in *DBAT* 16 (1982), 37-9

—, *Joseph und Aseneth* [JSHRZ II/4, 575-735], Gütersloh: Gerd Mohn, 1983

—, "Joseph and Aseneth," in-*OTP* 2:177-247

—, "The Importance of Joseph and Aseneth for the Study of the New Testament: A General Survey and a Fresh Look at the Lord's Supper," *NTS* 33 (1987), 102-34

—, "Der jüdische Asenethroman und seine Nachwirkung. Von Egeria zu Anna katharina Emmerick oder von Moses aus Aggel zu Karl Kerényi," *ANRW* II.20.1 (1987), 543-667

—, "The Present State of Research on Joseph and Aseneth," in-J. Neusner, P. Borgen, E.S. Frerichs, and R. Horsley (eds.), *New Perspectives on Ancient Judaism*, Lanham, New York and London: University Press of America, 1987, 2:31-52

P. Bureth, "Le préfet d'Egypte (30 av. J.C.—297 ap. J.C.): Etat présent de la documentation en 1973," *ANRW* II.10.1 (1988), 472-502

A.J. Butler, *The Arab Conquest of Egypt and the Last Thirty Years of the Roman Dominion*, rev. ed. by P.M. Fraser, Oxford: Clarendon, 1978 (1st ed. 1902)

A. Calderini, *Dizionario dei nomi geografici e topografici dell'Egitto greco-romano* (a cura di S. Daris), Milano: Cisalpino-Goliardica, 1972-88

D.B. Campbell, "Dating the Siege of Masada," *ZPE* 73 (1988), 156-8

E.F. Campbell, "Jewish Shrines of the Hellenistic and Persian Periods," in-F.M. Cross (ed.), *Symposia Celebrating the 75th Anniversary of ASOR*, Cambridge: American Society of Oriental Research, 1979, 2:159-67

J.P. Cassel, *Dissertatio Philologico-Historica de Templo Oniae Heliopolitano*, Bremen, 1730

E. Cavaignac, "Remarques sur le deuxième livre des Macchabées," *RHR* 130 (1945), 42-58

M. Chauveau, "Un été 145," *BIFAO* 90 (1990), 135-68

—, "Un été 145-Post Scriptum," *BIFAO* 91 (1991), 129-34

R.D. Chesnutt, "Bread of Life in Joseph and Aseneth and in John 6," in-J.E. Priest (ed.), *Johannine Studies: Essays in Honor of Frank Pack*, Malibu, CA: Pepperdine University Press, 1989, 1-16

—, *From Death to Life: Conversion in Joseph and Aseneth*, [JSP Suppl. 16], Sheffield: Sheffield Academic Press, 1995

A. Chester, "The Sibyl and the Temple," in-W. Horbury (ed.), *Templum Amicitiae: Essays on the Second Temple presented to Ernst Bammel* [JSNT Suppl. 48], Sheffield: JSOT Press, 1991, 37-69

B.D. Chilton, *The Isaiah Targum: Introduction, Translation, Apparatus and Notes* [The Aramaic Bible, 11], Wilmington, Delaware: Michael Glazier Inc, 1987

H. Chouliara-Raïos, *L'abeille et le miel en Egypte d'après les papyrus grecs*, Joannina: G. Tsolis, 1989

E. Christiansen, *Coins of Alexandria and the Nomes*, London: British Museum, 1991

G.M. Cohen, "The Hellenistic Military Colony: A Herodian Example," *TAPA* 103 (1972), 83-95

—, *The Seleucid Colonies: Studies in Founding, Administration and Organization* [Historia Einzelschriften, Heft 30], Wiesbaden: Franz Steiner Verlag, 1978

J.J. Collins, *The Sibylline Oracles of Egyptian Judaism*, [SBLDS 13], Missoula, Montana: University of Montana Press, 1974

—, "The Epic of Theodotus and the Hellenism of the Hasmoneans," *HTR* 73 (1980), 91-104

—, "The Sibylline oracles," in-*OTP* 1:317-472

—, *Between Athens and Jerusalem: Jewish Identity in the Hellenistic Diaspora*, New York: Crossroad, 1983

—, *Daniel*, [Hermeneia series], Minneapolis: Fortress, 1993

D. Cook, "Joseph and Aseneth," in-H.F.D. Sparks (ed.), *The Apocryphal Old Testament*, Oxford: Clarendon, 1984, 465-503

E. van't Dack, W. Clarysse, G. Cohen, J. Quaegebeur, and J.K. Winnicki, *The Judean-Syrian-Egyptian Conflict of 103-101 BC: A Multilingual Dossier Concerning a "War of Sceptres,"* Brussel: Koninklijke Academie, 1989

S. Dally, "Ancient Assyrian Textiles and the Origins of Carpet Design," *Iran* 29 (1991), 117-135

M. Delcor, "Un roman d'amour d'origine thérapeute: Le livre de Joseph et Aseneth," *Bulletin de Littératue Ecclésiastique* 63 (1962), 3-27

—, "Le temple d'Onias en Egypte," *RB* 75 (1968), 188-205

—, "Sanctuaires juifs," in-J. Briend, É. Cothenet, H. Cazelles, and A. Feuillet (eds.), *Supplément au Dictionnaire de la Bible*, Fasc. 64B-65, Paris: Letouzy & Ané, 1991, 1286-1329

G. Delling, "Einwirkungen der Sprache der Septuaginta in 'Joseph und Aseneth'," *JSJ* 9 (1978), 29-56

—, "Die Kunst des Gestaltens in 'Joseph und Aseneth'," *NT* 26 (1984), 1-42

A.-M. Denis, *Introduction aux pseudépigraphes grecs d'Ancien Testament*, Leiden: Brill, 1970

J.B. De Rossi, *Variae Lectiones Veteris Testamenti Librorum*, Parma: Bodoni, 1784-5, [repr. Amsterdam: Philo Press, 1970]

R. Doran, *Temple Propaganda: The Purpose and Character of 2 Maccabees* [CBQMS 12], Washington, DC: The Catholic Biblical Association of America, 1981

—, "Narrative Literature," in-R.A. Kraft and G.W.E. Nickelsburg (eds.), *Early Judaism and its Modern Interpreters*, Atlanta: Scholars Press, 1986, 287-310

S.E.H. Doty, *From Ivory Tower to City of Refuge: The Role and Function of the Protagonist in "Joseph and Aseneth" and Related Narratives*, unpublished PhD diss., Iliff School of Theology & University of Denver, 1989

B. Duhm, *Das Buch Jesaia*, Göttingen: Vandenhoeck & Ruprecht, 1892

C.C. Edgar, "Greek Inscriptions from the Delta," *ASAE* 11 (1911), 1-2

—, "A Group of Inscriptions from Demerdash," *BSAA* 15 (1914-15), 32-8

—, "More Tomb-stones from Tell el Yahoudieh," *ASAE* 22 (1922), 7-16

H. Eshel, "The Prayer of Joseph, a Papyrus from Masada and the Samaritan Temple on ΑΡΓΑΡΙΖΙΝ," *Zion* 56 (1991), 125-36 (Heb.)

U. Fischer, *Eschatologie und Jenseitserwartung im hellenistischen Diaspora-judentum*, Berlin: De Gruyter, 1978

Fourmont, *Description historique et geographique des plaines d'Heliopolis et de Memphis*, Paris: Duchesne, 1755

W.M. Flinders Petrie, *Hyksos and Israelite Cities*, London: School of Archaeology, 1906

—, *Egypt and Israel*, London: Society for Promoting Christian Knowledge, 1911

—, *Heliopolis, Kafr Ammar and Shurafa*, London: School of Archaeology and Bernard Quaritch, 1915

P.M. Fraser, *Ptolemaic Alexandria*, Oxford: Clarendon, 3 vols., 1972

J. Freudenthal, *Alexander Polyhistor und die von ihm erhaltenen Reste judäischer und samaritanischer Geschchtswerke*, [Hellenistische Studien 1-2], Breslau: Skutsch, 1875

J.-B. Frey, *Corpus Inscriptionum Judaicarum*, Rome: Pontifico Istituto di Archeologia Cristiana, 1936-52 (vol. 1 rev. by B. Lifshitz, New York: Ktav, 1975)

A. Fuks, "The Jewish Revolt in Egypt (A.D. 115-117) in the light of the papyri," *Aegyptus* 33 (1953), 131-58

A.H. Gardiner, *Ancient Egyptian Onomastica*, Oxford: Oxford University Press, 1947

J. Geffcken, *Komposition und Entstehungszeit der Oracula Sibyllina*, [Texte und Untersuchungen zur Geschichte der Altchristlichen Literatur 23/1], Leipzig: Hinrichs, 1903

P. Geyer, *Itineraria Hierosolomytana saeculi IIII-VIII* [CSEL 39], Wien-Prag-Leipzig: Tempsky & Freytag, 1898 (repr. NY: Johnson Reprint Corp., 1964)

H.L. Ginsberg, "The Oldest Interpretation of the Suffering Servant," *VT* 3 (1953), 400-4

F. Glorie (ed.), *S. Hieronymi... Commentarium in Danielem*, [CCSL 75A], Turnhout: Brepols, 1964

N. Golb, "The Topography of the Jews of Medieval Egypt," *JNES* 33 (1974), 116-49

J.A. Goldstein, "The Tales of the Tobiads," in-J. Neusner (ed.), *Christianity, Judaism and other Greco-Roman Cults. Studies for Morton Smith at Sixty* [SJLA 12], Leiden: Brill, 1975, 3:85-123

—, *I Maccabees* [Anchor Bible 41], NY: Doubleday, 1976

—, *II Maccabees* [Anchor Bible 41A], NY: Doubleday, 1983

D. Goodblatt, *The Monarchic Principle: Studies in Jewish Self-Governmet in Antiquity*, [TSAJ 38], Tübingen: J.C.B. Mohr, 1994

R.P. Gordon, "Terra Sancta and the Territorial Doctrine of the Targum to the Prophets", in-J.A. Emerton and S.C. Reif (eds.), *Interpreting the Hebrew Bible. Essays in Honor of E.I.J. Rosenthal*, Cambridge: Cambridge University Press, 1983

A.S.F. Gow, *Thecoritus*, 2 vols., Cambridge: Cambridge University Press, 1950

G.B. Gray, *A Critical and Exegetical Commentary on Isaiah I-XXXIX* (ICC series), Edinburgh: T&T Clark, Vol. 1, 1912

F.L. Griffith, *The Antiquities of Tell el Yahoudieh*, London: Egypt Exploration Fund, 1890, (in the same volume as E. Naville, *Mound of the Jew*)

E.S. Gruen, *The Hellenistic World and the Coming of Rome*, 2 vols., Berkeley: University of California Press, 1984

—, "The Origins and Objectives of onias' Temple," *Scripta Classica Israelica*, forthcoming

Y. Gutman, *The Beginnings of Jewish-Hellenistic Literature*, 2 vols., Jerusalem: Bialik, 1963 (Heb.)

D. Hagedorn and P.J. Sijpesteijn, "Die Stadtviertel von Herakleopolis," *ZPE* 65 (1986), 101-5

R. Hayward, "The Jewish Temple at Leontopolis: A Reconsideration," *JJS* 33 (1982), 429-43

W. Helck, "Natho," *LdÄ* vol. IV (1982), 354-5

M. Hengel, *Judaism and Hellenism: Studies in their Encounter in Palestine during the Early hellenistic period* (J. Bowden, tr.), 2 vols., Philadelphia: Fortress, 1974

M. Himmelfarb, *Ascent to Heaven in Jewish and Christian Apocalypses*, Oxford: Oxford University Press, 1993

S.A. Hirsch, "The Temple of Onias," in-*Jews' College Jubilee Volume*, London: Luzac & Co., 1906, 39-80

F. Hoffmann, *Ägypter und Amazonen*, [MPER 24], Wien: Hollinek, 1995

C.R. Holladay, *Fragments from Hellenistic Jewish Authors, Volume I: Historians*, Chico, CA: Scholars Press, 1983

T. Holtz, "Christliche Interpolationen in 'Joseph und Aseneth'," *NTS* 14 (1967/8), 482-97

E. Hornung, *Conceptions of God in Ancient Egypt: The One and the Many*, (tr. J. Baines), Ithaca: Cornell University Press, 1982

—, *The Valley of the Kings: Horizon of Eternity*, (tr. D. Warburton), New York: Timken Publishers, 1990

P.W. van der Horst, *Chaeremon, Egyptian Priest and Stoic Philosopher* [EPRO 101], Leiden: Brill, 1984

—, "Jewish Poetical Tomb Inscriptions," in-J.W. van Henten and P.W. van der Horst (eds.) *Studies in Early Jewish Epigraphy* [AGAJU XXI], Leiden: Brill, 1994, 129-47

E.M. Humphrey, *The Ladies and the Cities: Transformation and Apocalyptic Identity in Joseph and Aseneth, 4 Ezra, the Apocalypse and The Shepherd of Hermas*, [JSP Supplement Series, 17], Sheffield: Sheffield Academic Press, 1995

G. Husson, *OIKIA: Le vocabulaire de la maison privée en Égypte d'après les papyrus grecs*, Paris: Sorbonne, 1983

D.G. Jeffreys, *The Survey of Memphis*, Vol. 1, London: Egypt Exploration Society, 1985

P.P. Jenson, *Graded Holiness: A Key to the priestly Conception of the World* [JSOT Suppl. 106], Sheffileld: JSOT Press, 1992

J. Jeremias, "The Last Supper," *ET* 64 (1952/3), 91-2

A.C. Johnson, *Roman Egypt to the Reign of Diocletian* [vol. II of T. Frank (ed.), *An Economic Survey of Ancient Rome*], Patterson, NJ: Pageant Books, 1959 (1st ed. Johns Hopkins Press, 1936)

M. Jullien, *L'Egypte: Souvenirs bibliques et chrétiens*, Lille: Société Saint-Augustin, 1889

U. Kahrstedt, *Syrische Territorien in Hellenistischer Zeit*, Abh. d. Gesell. d. Wiss. z. Gött. N.F. XIX/2, Berlin: Weidmann, 1926

L. Kákosy, "Atum," *LdÄ*, 1:550-2

—, "Heliopolis," *LdÄ*, 2:1111-3

A. Kasher, "First Jewish Military Units in Ptolemaic Egypt," *JSJ* 9 (1978), 57-67

— "Jerusalem as a 'Metropolis' in Philo's National Consciousness," *Cathedra* 11 (1979), 45-56 (Heb.)

—, *The Jews in Hellenistic and Roman Egypt: The Struggle for Equal Rights*, Tübingen: J.C.B. Mohr, 1985

—, "Political and National Connections Between the Jews of Ptolemaic Egypt and their Brethren in Eretz Israel," in-M. Mor (ed.), *Eretz Israel, Israel and the Jewish Diaspora: Mutual Relations* [Studies in Jewish Civilization 1], Lanham-NY-London: University Press of America, 1991, 24-41

H.C. Kee, "The Socio-Cultural Setting of Joseph and Aseneth," *NTS* 29 (1983), 394-413

H. Kees, "'Ονίου," *RE* XVIII/1 (1939), 477-9

H. Kees, *Ancient Egypt: A Cultural Topography*, (tr. I.F.D. Morrow), Chicago: University of Chicago Press, 1961

V. Keil, "Onias III - Märtyrer oder Tempelgründer?," *ZAW* 97 (1985), 221-33

G.D. Kilpatrick, "The Last Supper," *ET* 64 (1952/3), 4-8

E. Klostermann (ed.), *Das Onomasticon*, [*Eusebius Werke*, III/1] Leipzig: Heinrichs, 1904

A. van der Kooij, *Die alten Textzeugen des Jesajabuches*, [Orbis Biblicus et Orientalis 35], Göttingen: Vandenhoeck & Ruprecht, 1981

R.S. Kraemer, *Her Share of the Blessing: Women's Religions among Pagans, Jews and Christians in the Greco-Roman World*, Oxford: Oxford University Press, 1992

—, "The Book of Aseneth," in-E. Schüssler-Fiorenza (ed.), *Searching the Scriptures 2: A Feminist Commentary*, Atlanta: Scholars Press, 1994, 787-816

S. Krauss, "Leontopolis," in-I. Singer (ed.), *The Jewish Encyclopedia*, vol. VIII, New York: Ktav, 1901, 7-8

J. Kugel, "Levi's Elevation to the Priesthood in Second Temple Writings," *HTR* 86 (1993), 1-64

H.C.O. Lancaster, "The Sibylline Oracles," in-*APOT* 2:368-406

E. Lanciers, "Die Alleinherrschaft des Ptolemaios VIII. im Jahre 164/163 v. Chr. und der name Euergetes," in-B.G. Mandilaras (ed.), *Proceedings of the XVIII Int. Cong. of Papyrology*, Athens: Greek Papyr. Soc., 1988, 2:405-33

M. Launey, *Recherches sur les armées hellenistiques*, Paris: De Boccard, 2 vols., 1949-50

J.C.H. Lebram, "Jerusalem, Wohnsitz der Weisheit," in-M.J. Vermaseren (ed.), *Studies in Hellenistic Religions*, [EPRO 78], Leiden: Brill, 1979, 103-128

J. Lesquier, *L'armée romaine d'Egypte d'Auguste à Dioclétien*, Cairo: IFAO, 1918

L.I. Levine, "The Political Struggle Between Pharisees and Sadducees in the Hasmonean Period," in-A. Oppenheimer, U. Rappaport and M. Stern (eds.), *Jerusalem in the Second Temple Period*, Jerusalem: Ben Zvi, 1980, 61-83 (Heb.)

N. Lewis, *Life in Egypt under Roman Rule*, Oxford: Clarendon, 1983

J.H. Levy, *Studies in Jewish Hellenism*, Jerusalem: Bialik, 1969

M. Lichtheim, *Ancient Egyptian Literature, Volume III: The Late Period*, Berkeley, University of California Press, 1980

A.B. Lloyd, *Herodotus Book II*, Leiden: Brill, 3 vols., 1975-88

B.-Z. Luria, "Who is Onias?," *Beit Miqra* 31 (1967), 65-81 (Heb.)

Y. Magen, "A Fortified Town of the Hellenistic Period on Mount Gerizim," *Qadmoniot* 19 (1986), 91-101

J. Maspero and G. Wiet, *Matériaux pour servir à la géographie de l'Egypte* [MIFAO 36], Cairo: IFAO, 1919

M.D. McDonald, *The Prophetic Oracles Concerning Egypt in the Old Testament*, unpublished PhD diss., Baylor University, 1978

J. Mélèze Modrzejewski, *Les juifs d'Egypte: De Ramsès II à Hadrien*, Paris: Editions Errance, 1991

D. Mendels, *The Land of Israel as a Political Concept in Hasmonean Literature: Recourse to History in Second Century B.C. Claims to the Holy Land*, Tübingen: J.C.B. Mohr, 1987

R. Merkelbach and M. Totti, *Abrasax: Ausgewählte Papyri religiösen und magischen Inhalts* [Papyrologica Coloniensia XVII], Köln: Westdeutscher Verlag, 2 vols., 1990-1

Le Comte du Mesnil du Buisson, "Compte rendu sommaire d'une mission à Tell El-Yahoudiyé," *BIFAO* 29 (1929), 155-78

—, "Le temple d'Onias et le camp Hyksos à Tell El-Yahoudiyé," *BIFAO* 35 (1935), 59-71

P.G.P. Meyboom, *The Nile Mosaic of Palestrina: Early Evidence of Egyptian Religion in Italy*, [Religions in the Graeco-Roman World, 121], Leiden: Brill, 1995

K. Miller (ed.), *Itineraria Romana*, Stuttgart: Strecker & Schröder, 1916

A. Momigliano, *Prime Linee di Storia della Tradizione Maccabaica*, Torino, 1931 [repr. Amsterdam: Hakkert, 1968]

—, "Per la data e la caratteristica della lettera di Aristea," *Aegyptus* 12 (1932), 161-72

—, *Alien Wisdom: The Limits of Hellenization*, Cambridge: Cambridge University Press, 1971

—, "La Portata Storica dei Vaticini sul Settimo Re nel Terzo Libro degli Oracoli Sibillini," in-*Forma Futuri: Studi in Onore del Cardinale Michele Pellegrino*, Torino: Bottega d'Erasmo, 1975, 1077-84

J.A. Montgomery, *A Critical and Exegetical Commentary on the Book of Daniel* [ICC], New York: Scribner's, 1927

L. Mooren, *The Aulic Titulature in Ptolemaic Egypt: Introduction and Prosopgraphy*, Brussel: Paleis der Akademiën, 1975

—, "Antiochos IV Epiphanes und das Ptolemäische Königtum," in-*Actes du XVe Congrès International de Papyrologie*, Bruxelles: Fondation Egyptologique Reine Elisabeth, 1979, 4:79-86

M. Mor, "Samaritan History: The Persian, Hellenistc and Hasmonean Period," in-A.D. Crown (ed.), *The Samaritans*, Tübingen: J.C.B. Mohr, 1989, 1-18

B. Motzo, *Saggi di storia e letteratura Giudeo-Ellenistica* [Contributi alla Scienza dell'Antichità 5], Firenze: Felice Le Monnier, 1924

H. Musurillo, *Acta Alexandrinorum*, Leipzig: Teubner, 1961

E. Naville, *The Mound of the Jews and the City of Onias*, London: Egypt Exploration Fund, 1890

A. Nibbi, "The Eastern Delta," in-N.-C. Grimal (ed.), *Prospection et sauvegarde des antiquités de l'Egypte* [Actes de la table ronde... 8-12 Janvier 1981], Cairo: IFAO, 1981, 181-3

G.W.E. Nickelsburg, *Jewish Literature between the Bible and the Mishnah*, Philadelphia: Fortress Press, 1981

Th. Nöldke, "ΑΣΣΥΡΙΟΣ ΣΥΡΙΟΣ ΣΥΡΟΣ," *Hermes* 5 (1871), 443-68

D. Noy, "The Jewish Communities of Leontopolis and Venosa," in-J.W. van Henten and P.W. van der Horst (eds.) *Studies in Early Jewish Epigraphy* [AGAJU XXI], Leiden: Brill, 1994, 162-82

Olck, "Biene," *RE* III/1 (1897), 431-50

J.C. O'Neil, "What is *Joseph and Aseneth* about?," *Henoch* 16 (1994), 189-98

W. Otto, *Priester und Tempel im Hellenistischen Ägypten*, Leipzig: Teubner, 2 vols., 1905-8

—, *Zur Geschichte der Zeit des 6. Ptolemäers*, [Abh. d. Bayer. Ak. der Wiss., Phil.-Hist. Abt. N.F. 11], München: Bayerischen Akademie der Wissenschaften, 1934

W. Otto and H. Bengtson, *Zur Geschichte des Niederganges des Ptolemäerreiches*, [Abh. d. Bayer. Ak. der Wiss., Phil.-Hist. Abt. N.F. 17], München: Bayerischen Akademie der Wissenschaften, 1938

F. Parente, "Onias III's Death and the Founding of the Temple of Leontopolis," in-F. Parente and J. Sievers (eds.) *Josephus and the History of the Greco-Roman Period: Essays in Memory of Morton Smith*, [Studia Post-Biblica, 41], Leiden: Brill, 1994

R.I. Pervo, "Joseph and Asenath and the Greek Novel," in-G. Macrae (ed.), *SBL Seminar Papers* 10 (1976), 171-81

M. Philonenko, "Initiation et mystère dans Joseph et Aséneth," in-C.J. Bleeker (ed), *Initiation*, Leiden: E.J. Brill, 1965, 147-53

—, *Joseph et Aséneth: Introduction, texte critique, traduction et notes*, Leiden: E.J. Brill, 1968

—, "Joseph et Aséneth: Questions actuelles," in-W.C. van Unnik (ed.), *La littérature juive entre Tenach et Mischna: Quelques problèms*, Leiden: E.J. Brill, 1974, 73-6

R.S. Poole, *Catalogue of the Coins of Alexandria and the Nomes*, London: British Museum, 1892

B. Porten, *Archives from Elephantine: The Life of an Ancient Jewish Military Colony*, Berkeley: University of California Press, 1968

B. Porter and R.L.B. Moss, *Topographical Bibliography of Ancient Egyptian Hieroglyphic Texts, Reliefs, and Paintings*, vol. III^2 (rev. by J. Malek), Oxford: Griffith Institute, 1981, vol. IV, Oxford: Clarendon, 1934

Cl. Préaux, "Esquisse d'une histoire des révolutions Egyptians sous les Lagides," *CdE* 11 (1936), 522-52

—, *L'Économie royale des Lagides*, Bruxelles: Fondation Égyptologique Reine Élisabeth, 1939

H. Priebatsch, *Die Josephsgeschichte in der Weltliteratur*, Breslau: M&H Marcus, 1937

R. Pummer, "Genesis 34 in Jewish Writings of the Hellenistic and Roman Periods," *HTR* 75 (1982), 177-88

U. Rappaport, "Les Iduméens en Egypte," *RPh* 43 (1969), 73-82

—, "The Samaritan Sect in the Hellenistic Period," *Zion* 55 (1990), 373-96 (Heb.)

J.D. Ray, *The Archive of Hor*, London: Egypt Exploration Society, 1976

—, "The Non-Literary Material From North Saqqâra: A Short Progress Report," *Enchoria* 8 (1978), 29-30

Th. Reinach, "Un préfet juif il y a deux mille ans," *REJ* 40 (1900), 50-4

R. Rémondon, "Les Antisémites de Memphis," *CdE* 35 (1960), 244-61

H. Ricke, "Der 'Hohe Sand in Heliopolis'," *ZÄS* 71 (1935), 107-11

—, "Eine Inventartafel aus Heliopolis im Turiner Museum," *ZÄS* 71 (1935), 111-33

P. Riessler, "Joseph und Asenath: Eine altjüdische Erzählung," *Theologische Quartalschrift* 103 (1922), 1-13

L. Robert, *Études épigraphiques et philologiques*, Paris: Champion, 1938

—, "Epigramme d'Egypte," *Hellenica* 1 (1940), 18-24

G. Robert-Turnow, *De Apium Mellisque apud Veteres Significatione et Symbolica et Mythologica*, Berlin: Weidmann, 1893

L. Ruppert, "Liebe und Bekehrung: Zur Typologie des hellenistisch-jüdischen Romans *Josef und Asenat*," in-F. Link (ed.), *Paradeigmata: Literarische Typologie des Alten Testaments*, part I [*Schriften zur Literaturwissenschaft* 5/1], Berlin: Duncker & Humblot, 1989, 33-42

D. Sänger, "Bekehrung und Exodus: Zum Jüdischen Traditioshintergrund von 'Joseph und Aseneth'," *JSJ* 10 (1979), 11-36

—, *Antikes Judentum und Die Mysterien: Religions-geschichtliche Untersuchungen zu Joseph und Aseneth* [WUNT 2.5], Tübingen: J.C.B. Mohr, 1980

—, "Erwägungen zur historischen Einordnung und zur Datierung von 'Joseph und Aseneth'," in-*La littérature intertestamentaire: Colloque de Strasbourg (17-19 octobre 1983)*, Paris: Presses universitaires de France, 1985, 181-202 [reprinted in ZNW 76 (1985), 86-106]

A.-A. Saleh, *Excavations at Heliopolis, Ancient Egyptian OUNU*, 2 vols., Cairo: Cairo University, 1981-3

A. Scarcella, "La polémologie des romans," in-M.-F. Baslez, P. Hoffmann and M. Trédé (eds.), *Le monde du roman grec*, Paris: Presses de l'École Normale Supérieure, 1992, 63-71

W. Schneemelcher (ed.), *New Testament Apocrypha* (rev. ed. by R.M. Wilson), Cambridge: Clark & Co., 1991

C. Schneider, "καταπέτασμα," *ThDNT* 3:628-30

A. Schoene (ed.), *Eusebi Chronicorum Libri Duo*, Berlin: Weidmann, 1866

E. Schürer, *The History of the Jewish People in the Time of Jesus Christ*, rev. by G. Vermes, F. Millar, M. Black, and M. Goodman, 3 vols., Edinburgh: T&T Clark, 1973-87

E. Schuller, "4Q 372 1: A Text about Joseph," *RQ* 55 (1990), 349-76

J. Schwartz, "Recherches sur l'évolution du roman de Joseph et Aséneth," *REJ* 143 (1984), 273-85

—, "Cléopâtre et Aséneth," *RHPhR* 65 (1985), 457-9

S. Schwartz, "John Hyrcanus I's Destruction of the Gerizim Temple and Judaean-Samaritan Relations," *Jewish History* 7 (1993), 9-25

O. Seeck (ed.), *Notitia Dignitatum*, Berlin: Weidmann, 1876

I.L. Seeligman, *The Septuagint Version of Isaiah: A Discussion of its Problems*, Leiden: E.J. Brill, 1948, 91-4

P.J. Sijpesteijn, "Mithridates' March from Pergamum to Alexandria in 48 BC," *Latomus* 24 (1965), 122-7

—, "Flavius Josephus and the Praefect of Egypt in 73 AD," *Historia* 28 (1979), 117-25

—, "Inscriptions from Egypt," *CdE* 65 (1990), 122-5

E.W. Smith, *Joseph and Asenath and Early Christian Literature: A Contribution to the Corpus Hellenisticum Novi Testamenti*, unpublished PhD Diss., Claremont Graduate School, Calif, 1974

—, "Joseph Material in Joseph and Asenath and Josephus relating to the Testament of Joseph," in-G.W.E. Nickelsburg (ed.), *Studies on the Testament of Joseph*, Missoula: Scholars Press, 1975, 133-7

J.Z. Smith, *To Take Place - Toward Theory in Ritual*, Chicago: University of Chicago Press, 1987

M. Smith, *Palestinian Parties and Politics that Shaped the Old Testament*, NY: Columbia University Press, 1971

W.F. Smith, *A Study of the Zadokite High Priesthood Within the Graeco-Roman Age: From Simeon the Just to the High Priests Appointed by Herod the Great*, unpublished PhD Diss., Harvard University, 1961

A. Standhartinger, *Das Frauenbild im Judentum der hellenistischen Zeit: Ein Beitrag anhand von 'Joseph und Aseneth'*, [AGAJU 26], Leiden: Brill, 1995

S.H. Steckoll, "The Qumran Sect in Relation to the Temple of Leontopolis," *RQ* 21 (1967), 55-69

R. Stehly, "Une citation des Upanishads dans Joseph et Aséneth," *RHPhR* 55 (1975), 209-13

M. Stern, "The Death of Onias III," *Zion* 25 (1960), 1-16 (Heb.)

—, *Greek and Latin Authors on Jews and Judaism*, Jerusalem: Israel Academy of Sciences and Humanities, 3 vols., 1974-84

—, "The Relations between the Hasmonean Kingdom and Ptolemaic Egypt, in View of the International Situation during the 2nd and 1st Centuries BCE," *Zion* 50 (1985), 81-106 (Heb.)

M.E. Stone, *Signs of the Judgement, Onomastica Sacra and the Generations from Adam* [University of Pennsylvania Armenian Texts and Studies 3], Chico, CA: Scholars Press, 1981

R.H. Stricker, "La prison de Joseph," *Acta Orientalia* 19 (1942), 101-37

V. Tcherikover, *Hellenistic Civilization and the Jews* (tr. S. Appelbaum), Philadelphia: Jewish Publication Society of America, 1959

—, "The Decline of the Jewish Diaspora in Egypt in the Roman Period," *JJS* 14 (1963), 1-32

H. Tchernowitz, "The 'Pairs' and Onias' Temple," in-*L. Ginzberg Jubilee Volume*, New York: The American Academy of Jewish Research, 1945, 123-47 (Heb.)

A. Terian, *Philonis Alexandrini De Animalibus: The Armenian Text with an Introduction, Translation and Commentary* [Supplements to Studia Philonica, 1], Chico, CA: Scholars Press, 1981

D.J. Thompson-Crawford, "The Idumaeans of Memphis and the Ptolemaic Politeumata," in-*Atti del XVII congresso internazionale di papirologia*, Naples: Centro int. per lo Studio dei papiri Ercolanesi, 1984, 1069-75

D.J. Thompson, *Memphis under the Ptolemies*, Princeton: Princeton University Press, 1988

P.A. Tiller, *A Commentary on the Animal Apocalypse of I Enoch* [SBL Early Judaism and its Literature 4], Atlanta: Scholars Press, 1993

S. Timm, *Das christlische-koptische Ägypten in arabischer Zeit*, [Beihefte zum Tübinger Atlas des vorderen Orients B41], 6 vols., 1984-92

E.P. Uphill, "Pithom and Raamses: Their Location and Significance," *JNES* 27 (1968), 291-316; 28 (1969), 15-39

G. Vaggi, "Siria e Siri nei documenti dell'Egitto greco-romano," *Aegyptus* 17 (1937), 29-51

B.-Z. Wacholder, "Pseudo-Eupolemus' Two Greek Fragments on the Life of Abraham," *HUCA* 34 (1963), 83-113

—, *Eupolemus: A Study of Judaeo-Greek Literature*, Cincinnati: Hbrew Union College, 1974

W.G. Waddell (ed.), *Manetho*, [LCL], Cambridge: Harvard University Press, 1980

S.L. Wallace, *Taxation in Egypt from Augustus to Diocletian*, Princeton: Princeton University Press, 1938

N. Walter, "Jüdisch-hellenistische Literatur vor Philon von Alexandrien (unter Ausschluss der Historiker)," *ANRW* II.20.1 (1987), 67-120

A. Wasserstein, "Notes on the Temple of Onias at Leontopolis," *ICS* 18 (1993), 119-29

B. Watterson, *The Gods of Ancient Egypt*, New York: Facts on File, 1984

M. Wellmann, "Aegyptisches," *Hermes* 31 (1896), 221-53

S. West, "Joseph and Asenath: A Neglected Greek Romance," *CQ* 24 (1974), 70-81

R.T. White, "The House of Peleg in the Dead Sea Scrolls," in-P.R. Davies and R.T. White (eds.), *A Tribute to Geza Vermes*, (JSOT Suppl. 100), Sheffield: JSOT Press, 1990, 67-98.

J.E.G. Whitehorne, "New Light on Temple and State in Roman Egypt," *JRH* 11 (1980/1), 218-26

U. Wilcken, *Grundzüge und Chrestomathie der Papyrusurkunde*, vol I.1, Leipzig: Teubner, 1912

J. Wilkinson, *Egeria's Travels to the Holy Land*, rev. ed., Warminster: Aris & Phillips, 1981 (or. ed. 1971)

E. Will, *Histoire politique du monde hellénistique²*, Nancy: Presses Universitaires, 2 vols., 1979

H. Willrich, *Urkundenfälschung in der hellenistisch-jüdischen Literatur*, Göttingen, 1924

L.M. Wills, *The Jewish Novel in the Ancient World*, Ithaca, NY: Cornell University Press, 1995

C. de Wit, *Le rôle et le sense du lion dans l'Egypt ancienne*, Leiden: E.J. Brill, 1951

G.R.H. Wright, "Tell el-Yahoudiah and the Glacis," *ZDPV* 84 (1968), 1-17

F. Wutz, *Onomastica Sacra* [Texte und Untersuchungen zur Geschichte der Altchristlichen Literatur 3/11], Leipzig: Hinrichs, 2 vols., 1914-5

R. Yankelevitch, "The Temple of Onias: Law and Reality," in-A. Oppenheimer, I. Gafni, and M. Stern (eds.), *Jews and Judaism in the Second Temple, Mishnaic and Talmudic Periods* (Safrai Festschrift), Jerusalem: Ben Zvi, 1993, 107-15 (Heb.)

J. Yoyotte, "Prêtres et sanctuaires du nome Héliopolite à la basse époque" *BIFAO* 54 (1954), 83-115

—, "l'Egypte ancienne et les origines de l'antijudaïsme," *RHR* 163 (1963), 133-43

J. Zandee, *Death as an Enemy According to Ancient Egyptian Conceptions*, Leiden: Brill, 1960

A.-P. Zivie, "Du côté de Babylone: Traditions littéraires et légendes populaires au secours de l'archéologie," in-*IFAO Livre du centenaire*, Cairo: IFAO, 1980, 511-7

—, "Tell el Yahoudieh: Il y a deux mille ans, un temple juif au coeur de l'Egypte,"*Nahar Misrayim* 2 (1981), 5-16

—, "La préservation des sites pharaoniques dans l'espace urbain du grand Caire," in-N.-C. Grimal (ed.), *Prospection et sauvegarde des antiquités de l'Egypte* [Actes de la table ronde... 8-12 Janvier 1981], Cairo: IFAO, 1981, 117-8

—, "Du bon usage des traditions littéraires et des légendes populaires: À propos du Caire et de sa région," in-*L'Egyptologie en 1979*, Paris: Editions du CNRS, 1982, 1:303-4

—, "Onias," *LdÄ*, 4:569-72

Index 1. Sources

Bible and Apocrypha

Pseudepigrapha

Qumran

Judeo-Greek Literature

Classical Literature

Achilles Tatius		Herodotus		Plutarch		
LC		II.165	28 n. 46	*De Is. et Os.*		
III.24	23 n. 20	II.182	72 n. 23	31	90 n. 16	
IV.12	64 n. 1			*Quaest. Conviv.*		
		Hesiod		IV.5.2	59 n. 31	
Aelian		*Op*				
VH		442	9 n. 11	Polybius		
IV.8	90 n. 16			III.71	64 n. 1	
XII.45	10 n. 14	Homer		XVIII.51.3-6	66 n. 8	
NA		*Iliad*				
I.10	12 n. 21	II.484-877	66 n. 8	Porphyry		
V.13	10 n. 13			*De Abstitnentia*		
XII.7	59 n. 31	Horapollo		IV.6	71 n. 21	
		Hieroglyphica				
Ammianus Marcellinus		I.17	59 n. 31	Cl. Ptolemy		
XVII.4.12	36 n. 73			*Geogr.*		
		Itin. Antonini		IV.5.53	25 n. 32	
Aristotle		163	29 n. 49			
HA		169	26 n. 38	Strabo		
VIII.626a	12 n. 21			*Geog.*		
		Macrobius		XVII.1.12	46 n. 8	
Arrian		*Saturnalia*		XVII.1.27-9	36	
Anabasis		I.21.16	59 n. 31	XVII.1.27	23 n. 22; 36	
III.1.3	23 n. 20				n. 73	
		Notitia Dignitatum		XVII.1.29	99	
[Caesar]		XXVIII.42	26 n. 38	XVII.1.30	36 n. 73	
Bell. Alex.						
XXVI.3	35 n. 70	Pausanias		Tacitus		
		IX.23.2	10 n. 14	*Hist.*		
Collumela		X.5.9	12 n. 22	I.11.1	46 n. 8	
RR						
IX.13.3-4	14 n. 26	Philostratus		Theocritus		
		Vita Apoll.		XXIV.97-8	73 n. 26	
Dio Cassius		VI.10	12 n. 22			
XLII.41-3	35 n. 70			Varro		
		Pindar		*RR*		
Diodorus Sic.		*Pyth.*		III.16.6	12 n. 21	
XXXI.15a	23 n. 21	IV.60	12 n. 22	III.16.29-31	10 n. 31	
XXXI.17a	23 n. 21					
		Plato		Virgil		
Heliodorus		*Politicus*		*Aeneid*		
Aethiopica		293d	10 n. 13	VII.115	9 n. 11	
I.6	64 n. 1			*Moretum*		
I.30	64 n. 1	Pliny		47-9	9 n. 11	
VIII.1	66 n. 8	*NH*				
VIII.16	64 n. 1	XI.16.44	12 n. 21	Xenophon		
		XI.22.69	14 n. 26	*Oeconomicus*		
				VII.34	10 n. 13	

Index 2. Authors

Adam, Sh. 28 n. 46
Agnostou-Canas, B. 23 n. 21
Allen, T.G. 59 n. 29, 30
Alon, G. 38 n. 78
Amélineau, E. 40 n. 88, 89; 99 n. 40; 104 n. 12
Aptowitzer, V. 6 n. 8; 89 n. 11
Avni, G. 36 n. 72
Aziza, C. 90 n. 15

Baedeker's Egypt 23 n. 20
Baines, J. 27 n. 43
Baker, C. 11 n. 16
Ball, J. 25 n. 32
Bammel, E. 12 n. 22
Barns, J.W.B. 102 n. 6
Barta, W. 59 n. 29
Barucq, A. 26 n. 34; 28 n. 45
Bastianini, G. 34 n. 65; 38 n. 77
Beckwith, R.T. 58 n. 25
Beek, M.A. 21 n. 7
Bengtson, H. 31 n. 56; 32 n. 57
Bernand, E. 59 n. 31
Bickerman, E.J. 20 n. 2; 71 n. 21; 103 n. 7
Bodson, L. 12 n. 22
Bohak, G. 1 n. 1; 23 n. 2; 26 n. 36; 43 n. 6; 46 n. 9; 57 n. 24; 74 n. 27; 80 n. 13; 90 n. 15; 92 n. 25; 103 n. 10
Bonneau, D. 68 n. 12
Bonner, C. 59 n. 32
Braun, M. 48 n. 12
Braunert, H. 39 n. 85
Broek, R. van den 99 n. 41
Brooks, E.W. xi n. 1
Brooten, B.J. 36 n. 72
Brugsch-Bey, E. 28 n. 46
Bruneau, Ph. 95 n. 28
Bunge, J.G. 21 n. 7
Burchard, Ch. xi n. 1, 2; xii n. 3, 4; xiv and n. 5, 8; xv n. 9; 1 n. 3; 9 n. 12; 15 n. 27; 48 n. 10; 56 n. 21; 59 n. 27; 61 n. 39; 76 n. 1; 78 n. 6; 86 n. 3; 87 n. 6; 86 n. 3; 87 n. 6; 89 n. 11; 98 and n. 35, 36, 39; 99 n. 43; 102 n. 1; 105 n. 1, 3; 106 n. 4, 5; 108 n. 7
Bureth, P. 38 n. 77
Butler, A.J. 23 n. 20

Calderini, A. 25 n. 30; 26 n. 39
Campbell, D.B. 38 n. 77
Campbell, E.F. 13 n. 23
Cassel, J.P. 19 n. 1
Cavaignac, E. 103 n. 7
Chauveau, M. 31 n. 56
Chesnutt, R.D. xii n. 4; 1 n. 2; 17 n. 29; 53 n. 19; 55 n. 20; 56 n. 21; 87 n. 10; 102 n. 3
Chester, A. 102 n. 5
Chilton, B.D. 38 n. 79
Chouliara-Raios, H.
Christiansen, E. 39 n. 85
Clerc, G. 25 n. 30
Cohen, G.M. 24 n. 24; 27 n. 41
Collins, J.J. 20 n. 3; 38 n. 81; 48 and n. 13; 89 n. 11; 95 n. 29; 102 n. 5; 103 n. 8

Dack, E. van't 25 n. 28; 27 n. 43; 32 n. 58
Dally, S. 11 n. 15
Delcor, M. 21 n. 8; 28 n. 44, 47; 29 n. 52; 30 n. 55; 91 n. 17
Delling, G. 1 n. 2; 49 n. 14; 59 n. 27; 60 n. 35; 87 n. 10
Denis, A.-M. 86 n. 3
De Rossi, J.B. 91 n. 17
Doran, R. 6 n. 8; 103 n. 8
Duhm, B. 22 n. 17

Edgar, C.C. 26 n. 36
Eshel, H. 13 n. 23; 91 n. 18; 95 n. 28

Fischer, U. 59 n. 27; 78 n. 6; 102 n. 4
Fourmont, 28 n. 48
Flinders Petrie, W.M. 28 and n. 46
Fraser, P.M. 23 n. 22
Freudenthal, J. 97 n. 34
Fuks, A. 39 n. 84

Gardiner, A.H. 28 n. 46
Geffcken, J. 38 n. 81; 57 n. 23
Geyer, P. 98 n. 38
Ginsberg, H.L. 23 n. 19
Glorie, F. 20 n. 5
Golb, N. 39 n. 84
Goldstein, J.A. 103 n. 7; 104 n. 11

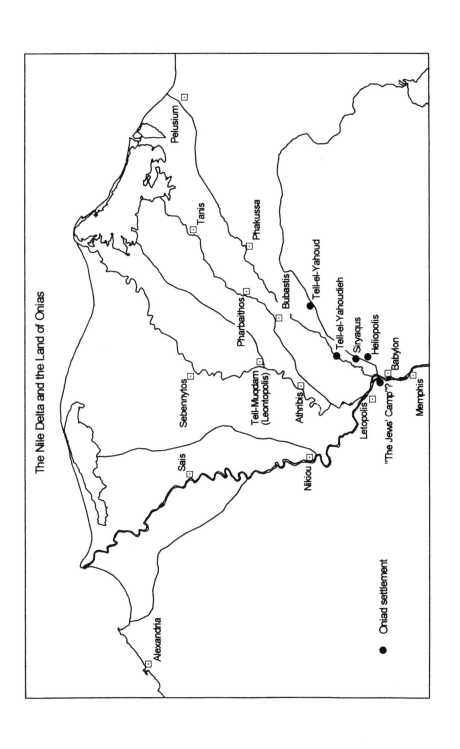

The Nile Delta and the Land of Onias

Pelusium

Tanis

Phakussa

Bubastis

Tell-el-Yahoud

Tell-el-Yahoudieh

Pharbaithos

Siryaqus

Heliopolis

Athribis

Babylon

Sebennytos

Tell-Muqdam
(Leontopolis)

Letopolis

"The Jews' Camp"?

Memphis

Sais

Nikiou

Alexandria

● Oniad settlement

CPSIA information can be obtained
at www.ICGtesting.com
Printed in the USA
FSHW01n1315090518
48039FS